$\mathcal{B}$ATHROOM

$\mathcal{R}$EMODELING

Hundreds of Bathroom Ideas, Styles, Designs,

Inspiration & Pictures

WORLD PRESS

Copyright © 2022 by

WORLD PRESS

TABLE OF CONTENTS

———— ◆ ◇ ◆ ————

Introduction

———— ◆◇◆ ————

T here are more than one good reason to decide to renovate your bathroom. In this introduction, we try to list some of these reasons and you may find out that the right time has come to create a modern and comfortable bathroom with Systems and Technology. This guide will work you through how best to improve this section of the home.

Optimize the space of your bathroom

We often like to have a spacious bathroom where we can move around safely without hitting furniture and bathroom fixtures?

Perhaps it is thought that increasing the space necessarily means masonry work to enlarge the square footage. However, even in micro-bathroom situations, it is possible to create a project by optimizing the arrangement of the sanitary fittings.

After a meticulous study, if the project is well executed it will be easy to position furniture and bathroom fixtures, obtaining more space with the same square footage. By moving, removing, or modifying the arrangement of the overall dimensions, you can change the look of your bathroom by giving it a new image and improving its comfort.

Create a laundry space in the anterior

If there is enough space, you may end up filling the bathroom with furniture, shelves, cabinets, and appliances. Without realizing it, precious square meters are sacrificed to the detriment of the convenience and comfort of this environment. Instead of creating a chaotic pseudo-warehouse, the best solution is to build a laundry room equipped with a washing machine, dryer, clothesline, and shelves.

Instead of putting everything in one place, you can create a new space where it wasn't. An anteroom, made specifically to cram household appliances and storage cabinets. The advantage is being able to enjoy a bathroom designed with furnishing solutions for an orderly and harmonious environment.

There is no shortage of technological solutions that home automation makes available, by installing interlocked power sockets.

These are equipped with a differential magnetothermic switch, which allows the plug of the appliance to be inserted or extracted in the complete absence of energy and therefore in total safety. It is the ideal product for humid environments such as the bathroom.

Replace the bathtub with a comfortable shower

Today, it is one of the most frequent jobs when it comes to renovating the bathroom making it practical. Especially when the home has only one, the bathtub is not the ideal solution for the needs of the whole family.

It is not just a question of convenience in using the shower cabin, but of a real change of appearance. Recovering space and optimizing the surface, gives brightness to the bathroom. When solutions such as the transparent or translucent glass shower enclosure are adopted, a feeling of modernity and lightness is instilled.

After so many years, it happens to notice that the style, the color, the shapes of our bathroom no longer reflect our taste. Deciding to renovate the bathroom with new bathroom fixtures, furnishings and putting a hand to the systems is not a trivial task. Following some practical precautions, you can renovate the bathroom without going crazy and without spending a fortune and following our advice.

Chapter 1: Things To Know Before Starting

The renovation of the bathroom is one of the least popular domestic environments, however, because maximum comfort it is always desired.

The bathroom, be it small or large must be organized in a functional anyway, however, choosing the furniture components should be based on the space available. In addition, glazing is also very important. Over the years, also concerning changing needs, it is often decided to renovate the bathroom; and here we will try to give you some useful suggestions to optimize time and costs.

Bathroom renovation

(how long does it take?)

It is not possible to answer this question clearly, because renovations can vary, be more or less complex, depending on the type of interventions to be carried out. One thing will be, for example, to repaint the walls and perhaps only replace the bathroom fixtures; It will be quite another thing, however, to carry out a total renovation, starting with the replacement of the floor.

In the first hypothesis, a few days will be enough, while in the second, the operations could take up to a week or so. It is therefore important to clarify that there is no standard time frame to renovate because each intervention will require more or less time depending on the work to be carried out.

Having said that, let's try to analyze some specific cases for the calculation of times. For the restyling of a bathroom that is not too dated and run down, the workers could take 2 to 5 days. If there are leaks that make it necessary to replace the plumbing system, then the work could last up to 6 or 7 days. Let's say that, on average, except for complications, the timing seldom exceeds 7 days.

Bathroom renovation phases

The restyling of a bathroom goes through precise phases, which we will try to describe in summary.

Demolition: It consists of the removal and rebuilding of all the components to be replaced. Very specific operations can be attributed to this phase, such as the removal of the floor and the dismantling of the screed, in other to be able to reach all the pipes, even the most hidden ones.

Refurbishment of systems: This is the second phase and results in total or partial replacement of the pre-existing plumbing system, usually opting for the most modern solutions on the market. In this sense, among the proposals, there are, for example, PVC or polyethylene drain pipes, to be chosen taking into account the respective characteristics and the connections of the sanitary ware that will then be installed. If the electrical system does not need to be replaced or does not require interventions, then you can move on to renovating the walls and plaster, arranging the tiles properly, if you have chosen them for the new style of furniture.

Laying of floors and sanitary ware: The fourth phase is characterized by the laying of the screed and floors. These are operations for which a particular skill of the workers is required to obtain a satisfactory result. In the meantime, the bathroom will be unusable; this can only be done after the time necessary to favor the drying of the cement and the taking root of the tiles has elapsed. Once the procedure is perfectly completed, new sanitary fittings and taps can be installed.

Testing: It is the last phase, a real litmus test, to verify that all the works have been carried out correctly. It is advisable that, in the presence of the technicians and not at a later time, you check that everything is working perfectly, starting with the taps. Specifically, make sure that: the water pressure is adequate, there is no loss, the sanitary ware is 100% intact, and the floor is not chipped.

If there are any observations to be made or disputes to be raised, it is advisable to do it immediately, without allowing days to pass from the delivery of the works. Also, remember that the cleaning of the room is always the responsibility of the company.

A tip for you: choose all the materials in advance to save time. We have seen that, although the cases may be different from each other, it is still possible to set a rough time for the duration of the renovation of a bathroom, which can usually last less or just over a week.

However, to optimize time, we advise you to choose all the materials in advance to have them already available as the workers request them. With this type of organization, you will manage your time better, without stressing yourself bouncing from one dealer to another.

Can I buy sanitaryware and bathroom furniture online?

Of course, it is worthwhile, first of all, to take advantage of offers at discounted prices, perhaps last minute, which you will hardly find by going to the retailer in person.

The second suggestion is to be wary of prices that are too discounted because poor quality could be hidden behind them. That's why, if you want to buy sanitaryware or bathroom furnishings online, first get a precise idea of the average market price, perhaps by going to a shop. Either way, buying online will allow you to search by brands, sizes, and features.

Chapter 2: Advantages And Disadvantages Of Drywall

———— ◆ ◇ ◆ ————

Pros and cons of plasterboard in the bathroom

D o you want to understand what plasterboard is? Do you have doubts if this type of material can be used in every room of the house? In this chapter, we will evaluate the advantages and disadvantages of using plasterboard in the bathroom, however, don't forget that there may be problems and also possible solutions to resolve them. What is drywall and where can it be used?

Plasterboard is a material that has been used in renovations (but also in new buildings) for about a hundred years. At first, plasterboard, especially in Italy, was seen as an inferior element compared to brick walls, but the presence of continuous innovations on materials, and its weak points, to make it a better product, is making it more and more used.

The plasterboard can be shaped to obtain structures such as niches or bookcases, which once finished will be perfectly integrated into the rear wall, thus guaranteeing a splendid result.

The plasterboard is made up of treated gypsum plates, which are inserted between two sheets of rigid cardboard, which serve as external reinforcement, there are standard sheets as width (120 cm) and of variable height depending on the needs of the work to be carried out (the, however, the maximum height is 350 cm). The thickness of the slabs will also be different according to the needs (slabs to be curved will be less thick than other slabs).

The plasterboard sheets can be subjected to various types of treatments:

1. Water repellent treatments (and therefore we will talk about waterproof plasterboard), to avoid problems in all those environments where we often come into contact with water, and therefore for use in the bathroom or kitchen, where

there is a risk that standard plasterboard is to have problems with mold, or that it rots.

2. Treatments to obtain fireproof sheets, therefore resistant to heat and flames, which are usually used in public environments, to reduce the possibility of fires.

3. Treatments to improve acoustic comfort to prevent the noise produced in a room from spreading to the rest of the house or to reduce external noise and ensure domestic quiet.

4. Treatments for thermal insulation reduce the dispersion of heat from one environment to another, thus obtaining excellent energy savings.

In addition to these specific types of plasterboard, there is also the possibility of using special padding for the cavities usually, the plasterboard walls are composed of panels mounted on a galvanized steel frame, which maintains a space between one wall and another. In this space, it is possible to insert different types of insulation (rock wool, polystyrene, or cork), to obtain thermal or acoustic insulation in this case as well.

Clearly, it will always be necessary to contact a professional to be able to identify the type of plasterboard most suitable for the type of work we want to carry out, to be sure of getting a job that corresponds to what we asked for.

Pros of drywall in the bathroom

Let's find out together the pros of plasterboard in the bathroom:

- Ease of making changes
- Soundproofing
- Robustness for suspended sanitary ware
- Easy to make

To create plasterboard counter-walls, as for masonry walls, long times and the use of bricks, or lime and mortar are not required: a professional can create the plasterboard wall in a short time, completely changing the appearance of our bathroom, for example by creating a new insulating counter wall, which will reduce the space in the bathroom but will make the bathroom more comfortable.

The procedure for the realization of the plasterboard involves the assembly of a galvanized steel frame which is fixed to the ceiling and the floor, and on which the plasterboard sheets are then fixed, cut to the necessary height, in case of too high walls or low, or in case we want to create special effects in our bathroom.

The whole process does not require the use of mortar or water, so the bathroom will not be excessively dirty. Unless you want to completely upset the bathroom, it is usually possible to keep the drains in their current position, also reducing the cost of the intervention.

Even if at a later time we will decide to restore the bathroom to how it was before the changes, thanks to the fact that the frame can be fixed to the existing floor with silicone, we will not have problems with tiles to change, while for the points where the frame it is fixed to the wall or ceiling, it will be sufficient to putty the holes left by the screws, without leaving any trace.

Although plasterboard is a fairly easy material to work, as regards the realization of plasterboard works in the bathroom, we recommend that you consult a professional, to avoid having problems with mold later on due to incorrect assembly, or wrong material choices.

Soundproofing

One of the most frequent reasons for installing plasterboard in the bathroom, especially in the case of renovations, is given by the fact that it is possible to create insulating cavities from an acoustic point of view: in this way, the rooms or rooms with walls bordering the bathroom will hear less all the noises that occur in the bathroom, such as a hairdryer, or someone pulling the water from the toilet, or the washing machine spinning.

This of course will depend on the type of intervention we are going to do, the case in which walls are built up to a certain height, to improve the aesthetics of the bathroom with the presence of steps or niches, clearly the acoustic insulation will be lower.

Robustness for suspended sanitary ware

The plasterboard in the bathroom still allows the use of suspended sanitary ware, the presence of the steel uprights on which the support plates to the sinks and suspended sanitary ware can be fixed, allows to create a modern bathroom with a sure visual impact.

For the assembly of these structures, the presence of drains and steel uprights must be considered, as the plasterboard alone is not designed to support loads of this type.

Clearly, the construction of walls and the use of plasterboard must be carried out by a professional, to ensure absolute impermeability and the correct use of the materials.

Disadvantages of plasterboard in the bathroom

Let's now discover together the cons of plasterboard in the bathroom. The disadvantage of plasterboard in the bathroom is more attention in the realization, while the cons of drywall in the bathroom are only one which is more attention in the realization.

As we have seen so far, the plasterboard, especially the waterproof one, is suitable for all works in the bathroom, from the creation of counter-walls for sanitary ware to niches that can act as an exposed wardrobe for towels and bathroom material, to dividers for showers.

Clearly, if these works are carried out with approximation and in an unprofessional way, the problems will become evident in a short time, with infiltrations and the presence of stains due to humidity.

For this reason, it is good to evaluate the necessary work together with the plasterer and the plumber, so that our bathroom is renovated in a workmanlike manner.

Still have doubts about plasterboard in the bathroom?

With this analysis of the advantages and disadvantages of using plasterboard in the bathroom, we hope to have helped you to get a better idea of what could be the characteristics to look for or discuss with a professional.

Chapter 3: The False Ceiling

◆ ◇ ◆

How, and why a ceiling should be suspended in the bathroom? There are three main reasons:

- Solve humidity and mold problems
  Create tailor-made lighting
- Improve insulation (both in terms of noise and thermal insulation).
- Regardless of the function it performs, the bathroom false ceiling should be made with special anti-humidity plasterboard sheets, coated with a thin water-repellent film.

16

The thickness of the cladding will depend on the size of the bathroom for the false ceiling of a small/low bathroom, you can use coupled panels to be glued directly to the ceiling, to create a barrier for thermal and acoustic insulation and protect the walls from environmental humidity.

In bathrooms with very high ceilings (difficult to heat) or with exposed systems, a dry false ceiling can be created, with a metal support structure, an insulating layer, and an external layer of damp-proof plasterboard. The prerogative of the dry false ceiling is that it can be inspected, to allow maintenance of the systems without breaking the coating.

If the function of the false ceiling is only to house the lighting, it is also possible to create small lowering or perimeter veils, which will cost less.

What is the cost of a bathroom ceiling?

Making a false ceiling just for lighting costs around 25 euros /sq m. Veils and lowering are cheaper, despite having a higher price per square meter (30/40 euros) because the price must be related to the surface.

If the bathroom countertop is used to combat mold and moisture, then some considerations need to be made. When the problem is only excess condensation, as often happens in blind bathrooms with an inadequate ventilation system, a false ceiling with water-resistant sheets and anti-mold paint is sufficient.

If there are real damp spots caused by infiltrations or by the capillary rising of the water in the walls, before laying the plasterboard the causes of humidity must be eliminated, to prevent the structural elements of the house from being damaged.

Finally, a factor that frequently determines the formation of mold in new buildings is the thermal bridges between inside and outside, which cause the walls to cool, especially near the edges. In these colder points, the water condenses easily, favoring the formation of mold. To avoid this, an insulating plasterboard false ceiling can be created, which has an average cost of 35 euros / m2.

A tip to save: The prices we have shown are indicative and may vary according to the materials used and labor costs in the different areas. Perhaps the simplest and most effective way to understand if a quote is convenient is to compare multiple offers. Comparing even just two or three quotes allows you to understand what are the prices of a plasterboard ceiling for the bathroom in your city; find professionals available to negotiate installation costs; compare multiple solutions based on the experience of professionals in the sector.

Integrated lighting

A distinctive feature of modern suspended ceilings is built-in lighting, of which there are several variants. Ceiling lighting can be widespread localized.

Diffused lighting can be obtained with a large central light, which however has the disadvantage of flattening the volumes of the objects and creating unsightly shadows, or with different light points arranged in a regular manner throughout the ceiling. For this last approach, recessed spotlights or LED strips arranged on perimeter veils can be used. Using veils with special recessed profiles, you can obtain the "light shower" effect, ideal for giving the bathroom a more intimate look.

Localized lighting can be obtained with adjustable spotlights or with recessed ceiling lights or led tubes. An original idea is to illuminate part of the false ceiling with path marker lights arranged in small rows. The false ceiling for the modern bathroom.

Are you on the hunt for bathroom countertop ideas?

First, you have to decide whether to leave the ceiling smooth or decorate it with lowering. The smooth ceiling is more suitable for small bathrooms, while the decorated one is more suitable for a large bathroom. The wavy veils are very scenic and also very modern.

Painting is important to give the right proportions to the environment. Using white or a very light neutral shade can help make the ceiling appear taller, a useful ploy in mini bathrooms. The colorful countertop helps make a scattered bathroom look a little more collected.

Choosing the right color combination can be a good way to restore proportion to a long and narrow bathroom or a bathroom in the attic.

A solution with a contemporary taste is to use parquet-effect coatings for both the floor and the false ceiling.

Need an idea for a rustic bathroom? The plasterboard ceiling can also be decorated with fake wooden beams, to be painted or left natural. For the lighting, you can use small "naked" suspensions, for a rustic-chic effect.

What about a minimal bathroom? Bathrooms without tiles or concrete effect can be combined with a white false ceiling with trimmer spotlights, to be inserted in small holes in the plasterboard. An original idea is to arrange them on the false ceiling in artistic disorder, only where needed (eg above the sanitary ware). Just be careful not to place them too close to the wall so as not to reveal the inaccuracies of the coating.

Chapter 4: Bathroom Windows
Choices And Advice

——— ◆ ◇ ◆ ———

I f you intend to renovate your bathroom, there are several elements that you must take into consideration in order not to make a mistake. Apart from the choice of furnishings, bathroom fixtures, and various furnishings, one thing that you must never neglect is the design and definition of windows and fixtures. The purchase must be planned with the advice of an expert.

Positioning of the bathroom relative to the placement of the house

If your bathroom will be exposed to the east, the light will illuminate it for the entire first half of the day, so you will need to provide a window frame that provides solar shading, to avoid the sauna effect in the morning, when getting ready to go out; if on the other hand, the bathroom window is exposed to the west, you will need to provide fixtures that allow good ventilation and the possibility of screening the windows in the long afternoon hours. To do everything from home and to know which windows and for how long they benefit from direct sunlight, you can use a practical online service.

Privacy factor

If the bathroom is across the neighbors garden or a busy street, you will need to consider this when choosing the appropriate window. Of course, the architect will take care of the aesthetic factor, but you should think of an automatic shading system to be applied to your windows. Finally, taking a relaxing bath, without fearing intrusive glances, will be a beautiful reality.

Making the most of natural light is a fundamental aspect, because, in addition to significantly affecting consumption, lowering it, natural light prevents mold and humidity, which are frequent in bathrooms and warms the rooms in a pleasant way. Here, too, the shading systems must be carefully planned to enjoy the benefits of natural light in a way that is protected from UV rays.

Types of windows: Spoiled for choice, bathroom size windows. The windows with tilting sashes, that is pivoting, horizontal or vertical, will allow a good level of safety if there are children in the house; the windows with sliding doors will allow exploitation of space especially in the case of small bathrooms; the highly versatile double-opening windows will provide plenty of air and light, allowing the upper or lower segment to be left open; the louver or grid windows will allow openings in sectors, also guaranteeing a good level of privacy; finally, the bi-fold windows, or with book opening, will allow a total opening with a very small footprint.

Material

Among the materials that are most suitable for the bathroom, we can recommend aluminum. Aluminum frames are made to last over time because the materials used are resistant to atmospheric agents and anti-corrosion; moreover, they have a low cost compared to other materials; not to mention the maintenance, almost zero. After installation, your aluminum doors and windows will accompany you for a long time, without needing to be refitted or treated like that of the wooden window frames; security is certainly a factor not to be neglected, both as regards the danger of fires and as regards the risk of burglary; finally, speaking of the environment, since aluminum is a completely recyclable material, aluminum frames ensure a high eco-compatibility index.

What to consider when choosing bathroom windows?

An element that you must NEVER neglect is the design of windows and fixtures. And let's talk about design because the choice of windows, both by type and by function, is a purchase that must be planned, perhaps with the help of an expert. Many will be able to rely on an architect as regards the design, but also relying on a professional for the technological consultancy of the fixtures will allow you to choose with peace of mind, be sure of the quality and durability of the product, as well as of the savings that will allow you to reduce the costs in the bill, thanks to the choice of the most suitable window.

What is your favorite style?

Whether you love the classic or the modern style, a window with aluminum frames will allow you to achieve that elegance you so desire; in fact, technological innovation does not necessarily mean stylistic ultra-modernity, on the contrary, quality fixtures manage to harmonize with any type of furniture, indeed, they even manage to enhance the environment in a discreet and refined way. In what position does your bathroom find itself in relation to the location of the house?

Chapter 5: The Choice Of Tiles

◆◇◆

D uring the renovation, it is essential to understand which bathroom tiles are the most suitable for our practical and aesthetic needs. Let's see in this chapter how to choose the bathroom tiles, considering that the surfaces of the room are one of the most important elements to give the environment a personal and original touch. From dimensions to bathroom tile colors, there are many factors to consider before making a final choice.

Bathroom tile size

The size of the tiles must be considered. There can be countless choices such as large, small, or mosaic. In addition to the unquestionable aesthetic taste, take a good look at the size of your bathroom and the height of the ceiling. Large tiles can give the impression that a space is larger than it is, and especially in low-ceilinged bathrooms, it can help make the space feel less cramped.

Bathroom tiles material

It is very important to choose bathroom tiles with a view not only for aesthetics but also for functionality. The bathroom is an environment that requires a lot of cleaning and the tiles must be easy to wash and resistant. Consequently, we must always consider the properties of the materials we are going to choose. For example, stone tiles have a tendency to retain more dirt than ceramic tiles, which are easier to clean.

Ceramic tiles are beautiful and durable and today they are the most chosen products for both the floor and the wall. In addition to presenting a huge range of color finishes and textures, they combine practicality, resistance, and versatility, as well as being non-toxic and recyclable. There are different types, each with its peculiarities, which may depend on the materials, processing, and cooking time.

We can find terracotta tiles which, depending on the clay compositions, are white or red. Single-fired tiles are those tiles made by firing support and glaze in a single solution, resulting in cheaper but lower quality. On the contrary, the double-fired tiles are made in two phases, first by baking the mixture, then by applying the glazes to the "biscuit" thus obtained, and then by baking the tile again to obtain the final product.

The "in body" porcelain stoneware tiles are not glazed and are obtained by pressing. They can be found in various colors and finishes, depending on the materials used, and have the great advantage of being almost non-absorbent, and therefore very suitable for naturally humid environments such as the bathroom. Glazed porcelain stoneware represents one of the most recent technological developments in the industry. These are tiles that have different colors and different textures and can give great freedom in the aesthetic composition of the environment.

Bathroom tiles which to choose for the floor and which for the walls

Floor tiles must be particularly resistant to wear, impact, trampling, and time, while those intended for wall cladding do not have the same requirements but generally must have more elaborate decorative effects. If the tiles for the flooring can also be used for the covering of walls or countertops, the opposite is to be categorically excluded.

Let's see how to choose the right bathroom tiles for the floor. First of all, you have to check is the PEI class. This is a classification that indicates the degree of abrasion resistance of the tile, which over the years is destined to come into contact with footwear, machinery, furniture, appliances, and cleaning products. Poor abrasion resistance can lead to aesthetic deterioration but also the material of the tile.

Which bathroom tiles to choose, then? The PEI index ranges from a minimum of 0 for the least resistant tiles up to a maximum of 5 for the most durable ones:

PEI 0: the use of these tiles on the floor is not recommended

PEI 1: can be applied in areas subject to a low level of foot traffic, only with soft-soled shoes or bare feet

PEI 2: they are functional for floors subject to medium foot traffic, with clean or lightly soiled shoes

PEI 3: can be installed throughout the house

PEI 4: ideal for all normal domestic environments as well as commercial ones with normal passage

PEI 5: functional to any type of environment, including heavy commercial ones such as, for example, large-scale distribution. For a bathroom, tiles below grade 2 should never be chosen.

How to choose the bathroom tile color

When the bathroom is small in size, it is better to choose neutral and delicate color tones. The environment is perceived as larger when there is greater brightness. Delicate tones such as beige are particularly suitable, perhaps with colored central bands to break up the monochrome.

Color matching bathroom tiles

The bathroom environment can be visually lightened with some tricks, such as combining bathroom tiles of different shades of the same color. To make the environment more lively and break the colors while maintaining a certain uniformity, you can insert tone-on-tone designs or decorations.

How to choose bathroom tiles (6 rules to avoid mistakes)

The options seem endless, but choosing the right tiles for our bathroom is possible, with a few tricks. When it comes to renovating our bathroom, the choice of tiles is fundamental, both from an aesthetic point of view and from that of functionality. From the floor to the walls, the surfaces we choose can have a strong impact on the room and give us the opportunity to give the environment a personal touch.

Selecting the coverings requires planning and many aspects must be put into consideration such as the size of the bathroom, the materials, the budget, and more.

It may seem like a difficult undertaking, but with a few tricks, the result can be surprising. Let's see some tips to deal with this choice.

1. **Size of the tiles**
   As we have already said, large tiles, for example, can make a room seem larger.

2. **Half beauty height**

   How high are the tiles to reach? A fully lined wall will give your bathroom a modern look. If you prefer a more classic look, you can stop at three-quarters.

3. **Cleaning and materials**

   The bathroom should be as clean as possible, and the tiles make everything a little easier, but you have to consider the materials. Ceramic tiles for example are usually easier to clean, while stone tiles tend to capture more dirt.

4. **Single focal point**

   In the choice of tiles, no one prevents us from having a little fun by adding a touch of color or a particular design. However, it is better to limit yourself to a single bold detail, while keeping the other coverings neutral.

5. **Three is the perfect number**

   If you want to create a more complex pattern, try to limit yourself to a maximum of three different types of tiles; one for the floor, one for the walls, and one for the details. Keep a single color palette to avoid a disharmonious and heavy effect.

6. **Without fear**

   While keeping in mind the latest tips, nothing prevents us from indulging ourselves. The choice of design and original shapes can only give personality to our bathroom.

Chapter 6: Renovating A Small Bathroom

A bathroom can be considered small when it has an area of less than 4 square meters (so it is not taken for granted that it is a complete bathroom, i.e. in which all the constituent elements are present toilet, bidet, sink, and shower or bathtub), how to renovate a small bathroom making the most use of the space and also managing to create the illusion that it appears larger? In renovating your small bathroom and then making use of most space, there are strategies.

Renovating a small bathroom: the strategies to adopt for the walls (sometimes unusual)

The first secret is to use colors wisely: shades affect the perception that you have of space, helping to visually enlarge it or, on the contrary, to narrow it, so soft and/or cold tones (such as blue) will determine the first effect. While dark and/or warm colors (such as red) will produce a shrinkage.

It is clear that this is a general rule because a lot also depends on how these colors are used, whether "pure" or combined with others, and on the tone that is chosen: different effects will be created using an acid green rather than a petrol green or bottle green.

Still, on the subject of coverings, it is not recommended to use small and square tiles when you want to renovate a small bathroom, instead favoring large ones with imperceptible joints, just as it is advisable to use the same type of covering for both the walls and the floor, thus managing to create continuity and fluidity in the color, without chromatic differences between high and low.

And speaking of strategies for renovating small bathrooms, once you have found the right coverings (the same for the floors too) it is not advisable to install them at full height, up to the ceiling, as was fashionable until the Eighties/ Nineties: better stop halfway up the wall or at 1.20-1.30 meters, or even plan to tile only the areas immediately adjacent to the water, i.e. the wall that houses the shower or bathtub, the one behind the sink, and the one where they are housed the sanitary.

Renovating a small bathroom (Tips for the Floors.): Two opinions have already been expressed regarding the walls: i. prefer large tiles instead of small ones, ii. opt for identical coverings for both dimensions; at this point, we also add another advice (valid for both coatings and floors), namely the use of micro-topping a material composed of a liquid polymer and a cement mixture which, once laid, creates a continuous surface, therefore free of joints, waterproof, and available in numerous color variations, the main advantage of which is that it can also be laid on existing tiles (therefore excellent in the case of renovating small bathrooms that must be made "economically" as they allow you to save on abatement and disposal costs).

Renovating a small bathroom (even the sanitary ware deserves attention.): To proceed with renovating a small bathroom it is then necessary to pay attention to the choice of bathroom fixtures: orienting oneself on small sizes, which the market is now teeming with, seems to us the right way!

As far as WC and bidet are concerned, the models that allow you to save space when renovating a small bathroom are those that are flush with the wall.

In principle, it is always good to choose everything suspended when you think of redoing a small spacious bathroom, because the more floor you can keep clear, the larger the room will seem, since the light can also filter under the sanitary fixtures and sink, giving more airiness to the whole, without neglecting the fact that maintaining cleanliness will be easier.

Still, on the subject of sanitary ware, and in particular of toilets, a further piece of advice is to choose an internal cistern which, if it fails in terms of maintenance (in case of leaks or breakages they are pains!), However, give a definitely better aesthetic, not interrupting the cleanliness and continuity of the wall: however, this is a solution that is not always applicable, so it will be necessary to evaluate its implementation together with renovation experts.

For the shower, the best choice could consist of a semicircular corner tray (which allows you to eliminate an edge) of dimensions not less than 80 × 80 (to avoid feeling a little "suffocated"), surmounted by a transparent shower box (which by not creating visual clutter it does not reduce the space).

The most suitable furniture for a small bathroom to be renovated. It is obvious that it is counterproductive to add too much furniture or too large (which it is true they will have greater storage capacity but "drown" the space), so after having said goodbye to the tub, too bulky, it would be advisable to choose suspended models also for the furniture, such as the under-washbasin furniture, next to which you can evaluate the placement of a vertical column, generally positioned next to the mirror above the washbasin: being also suspended, it will help to convey lightness.

Renovating a small bathroom (between niches and sliding doors.), other secrets to effectively renovate a small bathroom are to take advantage of the niches, if present, to install a heated towel rail or arrange shelves to create support bases and provide sliding doors and windows of the same type (or with vasistas opening) that do not they only allow you to gain space to move better, but also to be used as a design element.

Renovating a small bathroom (mirrors and lights): The most essential of the accessories is the mirror, not only for needs related to the toilet but also because it is a reflective element that helps to increase the feeling of spaciousness: for a small bathroom the most suitable choice is an oval or rounded shape because the elimination of corners in small spaces makes its contribution.

We have never seen a bathroom, no matter how small, without a mirror, and not even one without light ... but it is not certain that the one obtained is the right lighting (!). However it plays a very important role, as it does not have to be either too aggressive (remember that the bathroom is also a space dedicated to relaxation) or too dim or badly directed (because in this room most women are dedicated to make-up and facial cleansing).

Precisely for this reason, one could consider purchasing a mirror with integrated LED light, or a lamp to be positioned above the mirror (or 2 placed on the sides); for the ceiling, spotlights that can be adjusted according to need are the most desirable solution; while for the shower area you shouldn't be afraid to place the light (or lights) inside the box.

Renovating a small bathroom (which accessories to use?): In terms of accessories, we prefer those that are light and easy to move, perhaps equipped with wheels. We have already said that colors are by no means banned in the renovation of small bathrooms, provided of course that they are used wisely and wisely: an interesting strategy is to use neutral tones for the envelope (floors, walls, and furniture) and to play with the colors of the accessories (towels, toothbrush holders, etc.)

And in terms of accessories, we like the idea of the hydrobrush, useful for cleaning the inside of the toilet instead of the traditional one, compared to which it is certainly more practical, aesthetically more pleasant, decidedly more hygienic, but also more expensive (about 100 euros): once again the aim is to leave the floor as free as possible.

Are you planning or renovating your small bathroom?

A small room can express beauty and intimacy if it takes into account two key aspects,

- Making the most of space
- Make it look bigger

Choosing the right tiles can help you get the result you want. Whether it's a second bathroom, a guest bathroom, or a service bathroom, there is always the possibility of opting for solutions that enhance it and make it beautiful and functional.

Chapter 7: Renovating The Bathroom With Underfloor Heating

U nderfloor heating consisting of a system of radiant panels represents a cutting-edge technological solution that allows you to save on your bills and limit polluting emissions.

A series of advantages that has prompted not only many tenants, but also owners of offices and companies to turn to this type of solution also because, by increasing the energy efficiency of the buildings, you can also take advantage of a series of incentives and reductions of tax made available by the State and those for green renovations.

But every family and every person, of course, has specific needs and, perhaps, initially a limited budget or a simple desire to experiment with this technology in the first corner of the house: among other things, it is also a system that helps damp environments and subject to molds of various kinds, it can be very useful for the bathroom! Let's look at this type of context in more detail.

Bathroom and radiant systems

As we know, the toilet has, basically, a greater need for heat, since it must keep us warm during the shower, the bath in the tub, and all the collateral activities to personal hygiene.

On the other hand, to be able to relax or undress in total comfort without incurring thermal shock, especially during the cold seasons, it is essential that this room is suitably heated even before setting foot and it is precisely for this reason that it is necessary to think about a more ecological solution to be exploited, to avoid the waste that would damage not only the wallet but also the environment.

Underfloor heating is certainly an opportunity to consider, as it spreads the heat by exploiting the natural upward propagation, resulting in rooms with uniform temperature in less time and at low temperatures the water in the coils that run under the screed of the, in fact, tiles generally do not exceed 34 degrees centigrade.

Immediate comfort derives from the structure of the device perceiving the heat coming directly from the feet and radiating into our body, we immediately feel at ease and do not need to increase the power of the system (as happens, for example, with stoves, air conditioners or radiators) to defeat the feeling of cold.

All this can also be customized according to your needs: for example, it might be convenient to install a "towel warmer", also known as a "heated towel rail", that is a small radiator used for drying linen, given that towels and spongy fabrics in general, in winter, they struggle a little harder to stay without humidity. On the market, there are various types of materials and shapes and it is also possible to feed them directly from the hydraulic system (the same as the radiant panels).

Works (what to put on site)

Installing underfloor heating in the bathroom implies a temporary distortion of the room, even if it is an operation that can be easily inserted in a normal renovation situation: in fact, it is necessary to work on the plumbing system, lift the floor, install the coil and rearrange the screed and tiles to cover.

Furthermore, it is also important to know that this system should never be placed under the bathroom fixtures, the shower cubicle, or the bathtub and that, consequently, it is certainly advisable in sufficiently large rooms; indeed, it is precisely for this reason that the installation of a heated towel rail can become almost indispensable in certain cases.

Finally, it is established that there are no particular contraindications for the choice of the floor (even if the advice is to always consult in advance with the insider or a professional in the sector), there remains the enormous advantage also of furniture since the absence of bulky and aesthetically unpleasant structures allows great freedom in terms of design and furniture, which is no small feat!

Chapter 8: Natural Materials

— ◆◇◆ —

From coverings to furnishings, passing through the decoration, here are 9 ideas for renovating the bathroom with natural materials. The choice to use natural materials in the renovation of the bathroom can be dictated by the aesthetic taste, by the research on sustainability, by the desire for well-being that only natural materials can fully satisfy.

Imperfection makes them more similar to human nature and perhaps this is why we like the idea of using them, in particular, in the environment that we consider a "temple of well-being". Here are some examples of different materials and styles to experiment with if you are considering renovating your bathroom.

The wood

If we talk about natural materials for the bathroom, we can only start with wood, which with its irregular and always different grain is decorative and warm, as well as pleasant to the touch. Long avoided in this environment for its delicacy, today it can be adopted thanks to treatments and processes that make it resistant to humidity.

This is especially true for some essences, such as teak, which are more recommended than others for the bathroom. Within a project, wood can be used, as well as for the floor, as a furnishing element for chests of drawers and shelves.

The marble

Compared to wood, marble has completely different characteristics and one aspect in common: its irregular veins and colors make it unique in its kind.

A trend that has returned in recent years is to cover a bathroom wall in this material, choosing a neutral finish, for example in shades of gray, with a great decorative effect.

The Venetian terrace

In terms of trends, we cannot fail to mention the Venetian terrazzo, a material composed of fragments of marble and stone held together by lime or cement. Historically used for floors, it is back in fashion and also used with style on the walls.

The slate

With its dark gray tones, slate is among the natural materials that give a more contemporary and gritty look to the bathroom. It comes in different formats and finishes, from the roughest and most irregular for the walls to the smoothest for the floors.

It is a porous material that is treated to resist humidity and for this reason, it must never be treated with too aggressive products. However, it's very uneven surface makes it fascinating and sophisticated.

The stones

There are many other stones besides marble and slate that can find space in the bathroom. And not just as cladding, the stone can also be used for other elements such as, for example, the washbasin. It is a very decisive style choice which, however, involves a series of precautions in terms of use, since it requires careful maintenance due to the porosity of the material.

Lime

Lime is one of the oldest building materials and continues to be appreciated because it allows the walls to breathe. It derives from the processing of limestone rocks, which can take place differently and therefore lead to different results. In addition to giving uniformity to the coating, it is very durable and takes on slightly different shades of color over time.

The cement

The same effect of continuity can be achieved with concrete, a composite material with a natural base. It is obtained, in fact, by adding water to a powder of limestone and clay. The main difference from lime is the lower breathability. The effect is extremely modern, perfect for contemporary and industrial-style homes.

The pebbles

Small portions of the floor can also be covered with the appropriate river pebbles. Mounted on the net just like the classic mosaic, they are the ideal choice for a bathroom with a Mediterranean mood.

Preserved moss

Finally, even if it is not a real building material, stabilized moss is an asset for those who want to bring nature into the bathroom. It is not a live plant and therefore does not require special maintenance. Stabilization is a treatment that stops the aging of the plant as if it stopped time.

Bathroom decor can transform this often overlooked area of the home into a more functional, personal, and relaxing space.

An interior designer can help you come up with a plan that you'll be able to implement over time, with a budget that fits your needs, eliminating unnecessary stress and waste.

Why choose coatings in natural materials?

This is because the house is synonymous with intimacy and hospitality. This feeling has a precise reason. Natural materials are not tied to the fashions of the moment and, therefore, will never make the house appear out of date, "old", with an outdated style.

On the contrary, with "fashionable" materials, such as synthetic laminates, currently very popular for coatings and flooring, or ceramics that imitate other materials (the various "marble, stone, wood effect"), the risk that in a few years they will lose the appeal they have today.

Imitation coatings, while practical and inexpensive, are inevitably slaves to trends. Like all "fake" things, they are destined to be overcome by new fashions, tastes, and stylistic trends.

What looks trendy today will look simply dated tomorrow

Natural materials also have another peculiarity. They are able to integrate with our way of living the house and adapt with extreme versatility to any style of furniture. Wood, for example, goes perfectly with classic-style furnishings, with which it shares precious materiality and elegant taste.

In nature, however, there are infinite variations and essences of wood. By changing the chromatic point, the finish, the effect, or the format of the planks, the wooden cladding can enhance environments with an antithetical mood to the classic (contemporary or industrial for example), or create suggestive stylistic assonance with the rustic flavor of a country house or with the "unkempt elegant" of bleached oak furnishings and shabby details.

Chapter 9: Renovating The Bathroom

In An Eco-Sustainable Way

The bathroom, despite being in most cases the smallest room in the house, is the place where the greatest waste occurs. Just think of the fact that as much as 50% of the drinking water used daily, goes away with the taps and with the flushing of the toilet. If you intend to renovate a bathroom, you must take into consideration a series of measures that will improve the waste of drinking water. So be careful to reduce waste, but also to furniture, paints, tiles, and lighting.

As with any intervention that we put into practice on our home, even the bathroom renovation can be carried out with an eye to sustainability. Doing a renovation in a green way will not only allow you to reduce waste but also lower your bill costs and make you live in a healthier environment.

Here are some simple useful tips to renovate the bathroom in an ecological way.

1. **Toilet flush with double button**

   The old and obsolete toilet cisterns waste seven liters of water with every single flush. Today, however, it is possible to find on the market boxes with double jets that consume only 0.8 liters for liquid waste and 1.6 liters for solid waste.

2. **Nozzle for the shower**

   For the showerhead, buy low-flow or aerator sprayers, capable of delivering 2.5 liters of water per minute, compared to the 5-7 liters of common dispensers. This device also involves double savings in terms of energy required to produce hot water, since less water is supplied.

3. **Sensors on taps and bidets**

   For the sink and bidet taps, it is possible to install motion sensors, which interrupt the flow when they do not detect the presence. With this system, the waste of water is considerably reduced.

4. **Recycled ceramic tiles**

   Ceramic tiles are less prone to moisture damage and their impact on the environment during the manufacturing process is quite low. In recent years, tiles and bathroom tiles have been launched on the market that contains high percentages of recycled materials, to reduce the use of virgin raw materials and limit the production of waste.

5. **Led lighting**

As for lighting, during your bathroom renovation, it is better to opt directly for LEDs, which are more expensive than traditional ones, but which will pay off in your bill within a few months. The many people who have switched to this type of lighting have been able to see real cuts in the electricity bill.

6. **Ecological furniture and formaldehyde-free**

As for the purchase of furniture for your bathroom, it is better to prefer those made with ecological or recycled material. The wood used for the furniture must come from sustainably managed forests. It is advisable to avoid those that contain formaldehyde.

7. **Energy-saving fan**

If the bathroom in question is blind, then it will be necessary to install extractors or fans, making sure that these are energy-saving. Also, pay attention to how they will be set. To prevent mold from forming on bathroom doors, it is important to leave it running for up to 15 minutes after showering.

8. **Ecological paints**

If you have to redo the bathroom, remember to also choose eco paints with low environmental impact, mainly water-based, therefore not harmful to the environment. Recognizing them is simple, as they are marked with a special ecological quality label certified by the European Union.

Chapter 10: Renovating A Long And Narrow Bathroom

A long and narrow bathroom poses several problems in terms of the internal layout of the sanitary ware, not to mention the need to find an adequate space where to place a possible shower or bathtub.

The technical questions to be addressed change depending on whether the narrow rectangular-shaped bathroom is small if it has one or more windows, and finally depending on whether or not the sanitary fixtures need to be moved away from their arrangement.

In this chapter, you will find some solutions for the renovation of a rectangular bathroom that will allow you to make it more comfortable and spacious.

How to design a long and narrow bathroom

1. **Take the measurements well**

   To develop a project that allows you to improve the layout of a rectangular bathroom, you must first take the necessary measures correctly. You can do it with the classic mason's tape measure or with a distance meter. The important thing is that you note all the dimensions of the room, including those of any niches or protrusions, noting them on paper. It is also necessary to note the position of drains and arrangements for sanitary ware, any windows, as well as sockets and light points. The electrical contacts located near water must be protected in accordance with the provisions of the CEI 64-8 standard, which identifies various danger ranges starting from the center of the shower tray (the area of greatest risk).

2. **Pay attention to the disposition of the sanitary ware**

   In a small and narrow rectangular bathroom, the one that presents the most problems, it is often necessary to align all the fixtures on the longest wall. To comply with the law, however, the sanitary ware and the sink should have minimum distances which, among other things, are also those that make them usable! So, common sense in hand, the legislator reminds us that.

The toilet must be 20 centimeters from the bidet, 10 centimeters from the shower, 10 centimeters from the sink, and installed at least 15 centimeters from the wall. The bidet must be 20 centimeters from the shower, 10 centimeters from the sink, and 20 centimeters from the wall. There must be at least 5cm and 10cm between sink and shower between two twin sinks.

Therefore, the wall along which we decide to put the sanitary ware should have a minimum length of 80 cm. In these cases, it is always better to opt for space-saving or flush-to-the-wall sanitary ware, to gain precious cm both in width and in-depth.

The suspended or countertop washbasin allows you to use the space under the sink to create a small piece of furniture where you can put towels or cleaning products. There are also some just 50 cm deep, which develop in height or length. Where possible, it is advisable to consider the possibility of moving a partition wall to gain a few more cm in the bathroom and reach at least 120 cm, a length that would allow maintaining the right distance between the sanitary fixtures and to position them so as not to interfere with the door opening. If not, you will probably have to replace the classic standard opening door with a retractable or folding door.

3. **If you have no other options and the municipality allows it, take something away**

Finally, if the small and rectangular bathroom is a second bathroom or a bathroom in the bedroom, you can do without the bidet, compatibly with the building regulations of your municipality, by purchasing different useful spaces.

How to design a long and narrow bathroom (shower and tub)

In a rectangular bathroom with a shower, if the space available is less than the width of the standard shower trays (70 cm) it will be necessary to think of alternative solutions, some of which may be:

- Create a "pass-through" shower cubicle in the center of the room, with a shower tray flush with the floor and concealed protections in the wall.
- Create a shower enclosure with a window inside, if the short side is exactly where the window is. There are several solutions in this sense that allow you to create a rather large shower cubicle even in a small rectangular bathroom.
- Move the toilet a few cm to make room for a large shower cabin. Here too, if you want, we refer you to a specific study on the problems that can create the displacement of the toilet to the disposition of the drain.
- In a rectangular bathroom with a bathtub, the minimum space required for placing a standard bathtub is 170x70 cm. There are also small bathtubs, even quite cheap, which need a surface of just 105x43 cm and which can also be placed under a window.

How to save on long narrow bathroom remodeling

The costs of carrying out all these options are mainly related to manpower, therefore, to save money and be sure to have a job done in a workmanlike manner, it will be necessary to evaluate several estimates from specialized companies.

In our experience, three quotes are more than enough to evaluate the alternatives available in your area. In fact, entrusting this kind of work to firms working outside the area would entail an increase in costs linked to the need to pay the trip to the workers who make up the team.

In a few hours, you will have all the quotes you need to evaluate who to entrust the work to and to get an idea of the average cost in your area for the type of project you have chosen.

How to tile a long, narrow bathroom

The coverings in a long and narrow bathroom should be chosen based on two fundamental rules:

i.   Tiles should be light or neutral in color, with narrow joints to give a sense of continuity.

ii.   Decorations should be kept to a minimum and limited to one wall - usually the back wall.

To save money and make the spaces visually brighter, you could cover the existing tiling, if it is intact, with a waterproofing resin, using special stencils for decoration. A recent trend, for example, proposes to decorate the ceiling as well, emphasizing the particular shape of the bathroom, rather than trying to make it less evident.

The long narrow bathroom - or band bathroom - is often a heritage of the apartments of the past decades. When you need to renew it and it is not possible to change the plant there are tricks to furnish it to the best by exploiting its strengths. In this post, we see some of them.

You simply need to know how to furnish the long and narrow bathroom using some clever tricks to exploit its potential.

No. 1

Use The Wall At The Bottom For The Shower

Quite a common solution today is a narrow and long bathroom. Perfect if the window is not positioned right on that side (even if in 90% of cases it is just like that!), Preferable in any case even if there is a window (you just need to take precautions to protect it or opt for a non-compliant window. wood).

No. 2

Use the wall at the bottom for the shower

That's right, this is a little less common, original! Only possible and the width of the bathroom allows it. Whether it's a window or a French door, it's more comfortable if there's nothing in front of it.

The success of the walk-in shower is constantly growing and this is due to the fact that it breaks down all traditional architectural structures and creates an open space, giving a touch of greater depth to the entire bathroom. In other words, with the walk-in solution, the shower space remains open but, at the same time, imperceptibly divided by a glass wall that separates the shower area from the rest of the bathroom. In short, with a walk-in shower enclosure, you will combine the beauty of design with practicality, without having to give up anything in terms of appreciable performance.

It is a modern and contemporary solution, also known as an 'open shower' because its main feature is to have one of the sides completely free from walls. It is an open space shower concept, which eliminates traditional elements such as sliding doors, swing doors, etc.

Is the water splashing all over the place or not? In all honesty, we tell you that this risk exists, but for a very specific reason, the wrong design of the shower enclosure combined with its incorrect installation. Great attention must be paid to the slope of the shower box and, above all, to the position of the shower head. Important precautions, not to be underestimated.

How to get the right heat in a walk-in shower enclosure? Since this is an open space shower concept, it is clear that we must also think about how to ensure the right temperature inside it, especially in the winter season. Everything can be solved by evaluating the installation of a heated towel rail, to ensure a more concentrated and close source of heat.

Let's now take a closer look at the advantages and disadvantages of the most requested shower enclosure of the moment and destined to be increasingly successful.

Pros of a walk-in shower enclosure

1. Large space should be dedicated to the shower area.
2. Easy cleaning thanks to the few pieces of which it is composed.
3. Comfortable and safe shower environment also suitable for the elderly and children;

Cons of a walk-in shower enclosure

1. In some cases, small spills of water. We have already talked about this possibility previously, underlining that it is necessary to plan the shower area well, to avoid annoying inconveniences.
2. 'Open space' shower is therefore perceived as colder. To ensure a greater source of heat, especially in the winter months, we, therefore, suggest the installation of a heated towel rail.

Create A Darker Background

A patterned cladding, especially if it is darker than the other walls, makes the room deeper (if it wasn't already needed!). Instead of contrasting the long and narrow effect, it emphasizes it. As they say, "Befriend the enemy".

Shelves made in unexpected spaces, as deep as possible, just to support a small sink, are perfect for a secondary bathroom with the essentials for guests. Or even cabinets built into the wall, perhaps above the toilet positioned on the short wall.

Put The Tub Under The Window

Perpendicular or parallel to the long wall? It depends on the width of the bathroom. Or the position of the window and its opening (because often climbing over the tub to close it is not something for everyone here).

Chapter 11: Black And White Bathroom, Suggestions And Furnishing Ideas

— ◆ ◇ ◆ —

There lot of ideas and suggestions for a bathroom in these two colors, that is color black and white. The black and white bathroom is an elegant and refined choice to use any type of home atmosphere regardless of its size or style.

When choosing a bathroom declined in these two opposite colors, the first fundamental rule to follow is to evaluate the final balance of this room by considering it as a whole, including accessories.

Black and white bathroom, an elegant and timeless combination. Black and white are the two opposite colors par excellence that together create an elegant and timeless combination suitable for practically any room and living solution.

Minimalist black and white bathroom

Very popular in the fifties, sixties, and seventies, this combination, thanks to its extreme versatility, is experiencing a new rediscovery. Today it is proposed for the furnishing of bathrooms of any size and style.

Black and white bathroom, where to start

If you need to renovate a bathroom and you want to opt for the creation of an environment where you play with the contrast between black and white, the first choice you will have to face is that of the color to use to cover the walls and floor.

Then you will have to choose all the other elements such as sanitary ware, bathroom furniture, furnishing accessories, furnishing textiles such as sponges and curtains, and accessories always considering the alternation between the two colors.

The final aim is to obtain a black and white bathroom where these two colors contrast in a balanced and pleasant way without excess.

Floors and walls

The color of the floors and walls must be chosen by evaluating the size and brightness of the room in other to define not only the white or black color but also their degree of brightness.

Certainly, a matte black floor reflects less light than a glossy black floor and therefore can be better suited to small bathrooms.

Generally, in the creation of a black and white bathroom, a total black floor is contrasted with light walls in order to immediately play with this irresistible combination.

If your bathroom is medium or large and you love choices of character, you can opt for two-color or single-color tiles to be positioned in order to create particular geometric patterns

If the bathroom is small in size, it is preferable to choose single-color wall tiles, with black floors and glossy white walls that help make the room seem larger.

The sanitary

In most cases, the color chosen for the bathroom fixtures is white, but there is no shortage of black washbasins, toilets, and tubs that can attract their particularity.

Before making your choice, if it should be different from white, remember that the renovation of a bathroom and the replacement of the sanitary ware is a costly job from the economic point of view and that creates considerable inconvenience.

Therefore, consider your purchase carefully without acting on instinct or under the influence of the enthusiasm of the moment.

Bathroom furniture

Once you have defined the color of the floors, walls, and bathroom fixtures, you will choose the bathroom furniture. You have to evaluate the final balance based on the alternation of black and white. With black floors and walls, you can opt for white furniture whose lines will stand out from the dark background.

If, on the other hand, you have chosen a black floor and white walls, you can opt for black or two-tone furniture to continue and strengthen the alternation between these two colors.

Accessories

In a black and white bathroom, it is important to propose the alternation of these two colors also as regards the accessories.

In the case of dark furniture, you can opt for white one-color bathroom accessories or vice versa. In this way, you will obtain a final effect that is always balanced and elegant.

Furnishing fabrics

To complete your black and white bathroom it is also important to choose furnishing textiles such as curtains, carpets, towels, and sponges in these colors.

To enhance the choice of sponges by making them in turn become a sort of furnishing accessory, you can choose to store shelves or furniture with compartments without doors.

The black and white combination is perfect for creating bathrooms of the most diverse styles so that this environment integrates perfectly with the atmosphere of the rest of the house.

Vintage black and white bathroom

These two colors can be used to create vintage-style bathrooms. They are characterized by; tiled floors and walls, sanitaryware with rounded and retro lines wooden furniture with steel knobs.

Modern black and white bathroom

The black and white fit perfectly into bathrooms furnished in a modern style with floors and walls made of resin. This material is extremely versatile and easy to clean. Its installation does not include joints and escape routes that blacken easily and where dust and bacteria generally lurk.

Minimal black and white bathroom

For a minimal style, opt for single-color floors and walls and furniture with simple lines. In these cases, the advice is to reduce the visible accessories to a minimum. You can remedy the criticality of an excessive coldness of the environment with the inclusion of some green plants.

Black and white bathroom (mistakes to avoid)

When decorating a bathroom in these colors it is important not to make the following mistakes.

1. Create an excessive and exaggerated alternation of the two colors that can annoy the eye.
2. Exceeding with black making a bathroom visually smaller.
3. Exceeding with black and creating a bathroom with a gloomy atmosphere.
4. Create a bathroom with a cold and not very relaxing atmosphere

By following our advice you will obtain a balanced and pleasant final result regardless of the chosen furnishing style

Chapter 12: How To Choose The

Bathroom Style

I f you are moving to a new home or considering renovating a bathroom, the thought alone can be daunting in itself. Don't worry, see it as an opportunity to create another room in the house that can benefit from your personal touch and become an extension of your being. Unleash your inclinations and choose the bathroom style that most fascinates you by following our advice.

Be inspired by your identity

Think about the styles you like best, not necessarily in the décor. Take inspiration from your wardrobe, the garden, or even the reading you love. You are romantic? Rather cold? Do you love cuddles? Try using the bathroom remodel as an opportunity to express that part of yourself that you like and want to bring to the fore.

Don't just take a cue from magazines

Furniture magazines are useful for getting ideas, but sometimes what is shown in the images is so glossy that it is intimidating and discouraging. Search for what is accessible and achievable, visit corporate showrooms, be inspired by elegant hotels, trendy restaurants, and even friends' houses. Take pictures and create a sort of bulletin board made up of all those elements that impressed you the most.

Take into account the spaces

It is important to know exactly how much space you have when designing a bathroom. A designer or architect can make a drawing to scale, or you can create your own using graph paper. The project will help you understand where essential elements such as the tub, shower, toilet, and sink can be placed. You should also take into account the location of doors and windows. Even a very small bathroom can be transformed into a welcoming and functional space thanks to careful planning. For example, consider installing a wall-mounted sink that will help you save valuable floor space. If the spaces are very large you can create separate areas for him and her, with a great visual impact. Remember that colors, lines, textures, and bathroom furnishings all play a visually important role in the size of this home environment.

Tiles and coverings set the tone in the bathroom

The choice of tiles and coverings is delicate because the general tone that your bathroom will take on depends on these. The small white metropolitan style tile is easy to clean and gives brightness to the environment, but it is a style element typical of industrial bathrooms. The same goes for gray or very dark tiles, which should be inserted in industrial-style bathrooms. Smooth ceramic can be found in a rainbow of colors, cleans just as quickly, and can fit pretty well with any style. Stone gives the bathroom a rustic yet extremely sophisticated look, while glass gives it a modern look. Play with a color change of the tiles to highlight an area. For example, you could use white tiles everywhere and visually define the shower cubicle area with colored tiles.

Choose the right floor

Never use tiles designed for walls, as they are unsuitable. Porcelain stoneware is practical, resistant, and easy to maintain. This material reproduces the look of stone or wood very well. The natural stone floor has an elegant, timeless appearance and is very durable. Rubber is a good choice for a bathroom used by young children. It is also ideal in the event of a fall. The high-quality PVC flooring feels comfortable and warm underfoot. It can resemble stone or wood and is available in numerous shades. Laminate floors are easy to maintain. Finally, the classic wooden parquet gives a feeling of well-being, it goes well with the minimalist style, but also with a more modern bathroom style.

Wallpaper

The wallpaper is by no means obsolete, quite the opposite! It is increasingly found in luxury homes. It should be applied on a single wall or on the ceiling to have a bathroom with a strong personality and a strong visual impact, or on all walls to have a more traditional look. Better to apply it on a single wall when the wallpaper theme is very strong, if it were put on all four walls it could create a feeling of oppression and heaviness. It must be in TNT or, even better, in glass fibers because they are 100% waterproof. The advantage of wallpaper is that it has great furnishing power: it creates a style, personalizing the environment more strongly and immediately than traditional bathroom furniture.

Focus on the taps

The faucet in the bathroom is a bit like the icing on the cake. If you've always dreamed of a washbasin with a wall-mounted tap, this is the right time to make your dream come true. Faucets, mixers, and mixers must be chosen in line with the style of the sink, which is the main and most visible piece of the bathroom. They can be chromed, satin, copper, or bronze, with minimal lines or a sophisticated look. The essential thing is that the taps coordinate perfectly with the bathroom furnishing style.

Strong style knobs and handles

If the bathroom has a classic style, we recommend that you visit some antique shops or find a craftsman to have knobs and handles made with a unique design.

Choice of bathroom accessories

Choosing accessories is probably the easiest and most fun part because the possibilities are endless. You can find several in each price range.

However, they must be chosen with great care, based on the style you want to give to the bathroom. Prefer simple and linear lines, accessories made of glass, resin, and ceramic for modern style bathrooms.

Choose rounded and geometric lines, with details in wood or stone, if the bathroom is made in Zen style.

Here are some of the most popular bathroom interior design styles. Find out what characterizes them and let yourself be inspired by the one that best suits your personality and your inclinations.

Farm style

This style of interior design is characterized by few accessories and a lot of attention to simple but robust materials such as wood. To achieve this style, many use second-hand furniture, freestanding bathtubs, painted finishes, vintage lights, and mirrors.

Contemporary style

Clean lines characterize this style. There are no architectural ornaments such as moldings or face mirrors on the cabinets. The cleanliness of the design is also reflected in the lack of clutter. The focus is on elegant materials and simple and essential lighting to create a refined atmosphere. Materials such as polished steel, glass, ceramic, but also stone and marble, are the masters in this style.

Asian style

Even the bathroom can be inspired by the typical atmospheres of distant Asia. This style draws on oriental tradition and design to create a kind of spa-like sanctuary. The soft lighting, the abundant wood everywhere, the minimalist design, the use of natural stone and ornamental plants, immediately create a relaxing environment, almost a place for meditation.

Traditional style

Beware, it would be a mistake to confuse this style for something that tastes old or outdated.

The traditional style celebrates classic materials and designs that have stood the test of time. It is characterized by the presence of many details, abundant furniture made of sturdy wooden cabinets and cabinets, and rich in mirrors and decorations.

Other elements characterizing this style are also the tiles, the antique appliques, the relaxing colors, and the elegant materials such as marble.

Industrial style

If you love roughness, the industrial style is for you. Raw and sturdy materials like brick, concrete, and steel bring this style to life. It is increasingly common to find these finishes in the lofts of large cities and industrial buildings transformed into condominiums. The industrial style bathroom is functional, robust, and has a very strong personality.

Mediterranean style

Just like the Mediterranean diet, this style gives the bathroom a sunny look, a feeling of lightness and happiness. Vibrant colors and intricately patterned and colorful tiles, arches, ornate mirrors, and burnished metals are just some of the features of this very airy style.

Chapter 13: Contemporary Style

◆◇◆

H alfway between the purely classic style and the modern style is the contemporary style. This type of furniture has as a guideline for the maximum and perfect realization of its peak of beauty two essential characteristics that must never be denied: the creation of simple and minimalist lines and a preference for accessories in step with the times.

To put it briefly, it is a style that is close to the very modern but which must maintain its somewhat classical linearity without going beyond the limits of the too traditional. A style with a defined balance can become precarious if its specific characteristics are not respected.

1. **Sanitary ware (type and material)**

   Ceramic is the perfect and suitable material for a contemporary style, a classic material that responds exactly to the linear and essential needs required.

   The "suspended" models are the most suitable for your bathroom. Their particular shape guarantees that essentiality, given by their being compact and above all simple. Choosing the right bathroom fixtures, essential elements of your bathroom, are the first step to lead you to the perfect style.

2. **Bath or Shower (recreates a spa-style)**

   The linearity of style matches perfectly with that of wellness centers and spas. In your contemporary bathroom, minimal but with character, a shower enclosure with one side to the wall and the other 3 glass or crystal walls would fit well, so as not to affect the spatial depth.

   If, on the other hand, you are a bathtub type, try not to occupy the central space, not to fill every hole at random: choose the built-in or corner models. In this way, you can create linearity and continuity with the walls of your bathroom.

3. **Furniture and shelves (respect the spaces)**

   The simple and essential lines of the contemporary style indirectly claim an airy and decidedly space-saving space. If you also imagine your bathroom as a closet or a storage room, then contemporary style is not for you.

Spaces are a very important element for a contemporary aesthetic, so don't suffocate your space. Choose countertop shelves to store all that is necessary for the care of your daily cleaning and beauty. This is not to say that furniture is banned, also because daily linen must have a "place" to stay. You have two style options: either suspended furniture, which also gives the right completeness to your bathroom fixture set, or opts for vanity units, which reflect the contemporary style lines.

4. **Floors and walls (watch out for color)**

   Let's move on to carefully choose the walls and floors to insert in your bathroom and above all the colors to choose.

   Regarding the colors, the natural, simple and soft ones are perfect. Avoid floors that are too thick or with eccentric prints. You also prefer concrete and wood effect, which are the best for your contemporary bathroom.

By following our guidelines, you will have a bathroom with a perfect contemporary style.

How to furnish a bathroom in a classic contemporary style?

We know well that the neoclassical style means elegance and luxury even in the bathroom, but that it takes good taste to create a perfect one. In order not to be mistaken, it is better to remain sober, choosing a few elements, only two or three more refined details, to give the bathroom that touch of timeless elegance.

Creating a classic and elegant bathroom does not mean looking only at the past. The secret is to reinterpret the typical elegance of classic design in a modern way to make it more current. You have to carefully choose the right furnishings, be able to customize the bathroom freestanding bathtubs, sinks, mirrors, and refined design finishes, and place them in the right place to make them the focal point of the room.

Let's see what are the key elements not to be overlooked!

Relaxing mood

The contemporary classic bathrooms feel more like a relaxing oasis, with an aesthetic of elegant shades and super luxury touches. Generally, they take their cue from what is currently trendy in the world of design, but choose timeless finishes and decorations, with clean lines.

The most interesting feature of this style is that you can mix and match the eras, without appearing visually cluttered. You can measure how classic and how contemporary it is, so it's truly a versatile style that never tires.

The tones of the coverings and furnishings are mostly light, especially in the case of small to medium-sized bathrooms. It generally works to combine a marble effect with wood or with another darker marble tone.

Remember that you don't have to choose many materials because this is not the "tile fair"! The decoration is a mix of flair and style, like dressing up with elegance or setting a table.

The main intent is to be enveloped in an almost suspended dimension, an aura created with the masterful use of colors and volumes.

- Furnishing a bathroom in a classic contemporary style of the materials.
- Choose materials that are as natural as possible. Wood is typically used for furniture bases or floors.
- The washbasins are typically made of stone or ceramic, but we do not disdain the more contemporary combinations, in composite stones. The most commonly used types of sinks are freestanding or countertop, to always make the shape of the sink itself visible.
- If you choose to insert a bathtub, built-in, or the classic bathtub with porcelain feet, you can also find solutions in a wide variety of materials to imitate the look of porcelain such as cast iron, cristalplant, or acrylic.
- Metals are key to maintaining a traditional aesthetic. They are a great choice for chandeliers, faucets, drawer handles, and even trims around mirrors.
- The most common metals are brushed bronze, iron, and copper, but also gold in the most extreme cases, which provides a touch of beauty and historical authenticity to your

design. But remember that the more extreme the design, the harder it will be to maintain a timeless look.

The coatings

A self-respecting classic contemporary bathroom must have a touch of polish. Certainly, it is easier to make it a coating.

The leading classic materials are marble, stone, and ceramic. Not only do they provide a sense of luxury and quality, but they are also strong, durable, and easy to maintain. The large slabs, those exceeding 270cm in height, are able to give a truly extraordinary look. There are large slabs on the market that guarantee the continuity of the grain. The result is a wall completely made of marble as if it were a single slab of more than 4 meters. A show!

Another interesting coating is wood or marble laid in a chevron, herringbone pattern. This is an extra refinement detail that lasts for years!

Colors

If you want a traditional bathroom that is chic and timeless, consider opting for a light gray or white scheme - this solid color can be broken up with the addition of wainscoting or wood flooring. Pair with white sanitary ware and bathroom accessories for a super relaxing space.

White is an excellent background against which various focal points or color accents can be created using smaller details, such as linens or bathroom accessories.

Attention to details

The contemporary classic bathroom must have an interesting focal point. It can be a freestanding tub or a change of liner in the shower, but details are always key to this design.

I love the elegant vibe of a period bathroom, especially if with unobtainable details like stacked logs or an original fireplace.

Great research needs to be done for bathroom furniture. Today wooden rigatini are very fashionable, they are very elegant and give an unprecedented vibration to the bathroom.

Get inspired!

Chapter 14: The Bathroom In A Modern Style

Modern style bathrooms are among the most requested during renovations, this is because the modern style offers aesthetically striking solutions, but is also practical and functional, allowing you to optimize spaces and make the most of the functionality of the furnishings.

Furthermore, with their furnishing solutions, modern bathrooms also adapt to particular situations such as small bathrooms or blind bathrooms, allowing you to make the most of these environments, despite the disadvantages associated with their characteristics.

The watchwords of a modern style bathroom are geometry and minimalism. Modern furniture favors essentiality which corresponds in the furnishings to geometric and clean lines, accessories limited to essentiality, neutral colors with the possibility of livening up the environment with contrasting spot colors.

For the walls of a modern bathroom it is good to limit the use of tiles: no to classic tiles with floral or colored motifs, yes to inserts, mosaic tiles, tiles of particular shapes and sizes in neutral colors.

A very popular solution for the walls of modern bathrooms is to use walls without coverings painted in neutral colors such as gray, ice, dove gray.

For the floors, light parquet floors are particularly suitable, as well as natural materials such as slate, porcelain stoneware, and marble in the cases of modern bathrooms that aim for an elegant and luxurious effect.

Finally, for the surfaces, you can use materials such as wood, natural materials, stone, marble, okite, and other types of coatings.

The washbasins and sanitary fixtures of a modern bathroom also follow essential, geometric, but above all harmonious lines.

As for the washbasins, which can be single or double, the shapes can be square, elliptical, or irregular, but always harmonized with the rest of the furniture. Lately a very popular trend to furnish the bathroom in a modern style is to place the washbasins so that they rest on the furniture, often made of light wood, thus creating a very pleasant chromatic effect with the white of the ceramic.

For sanitary ware, consider suspended sanitary ware, which usually comes in white, but can often also be made in black or even steel.

The most used showers for modern bathrooms are very essential walk-in showers, with square shapes and high-transparency glass, while as regards the bathtubs, there are several design proposals for modern bathroom furnishings: from the elliptical whirlpool tub, circular or with an irregular shape, up to the modern reinterpretation of the old tubs with feet, true masterpieces of contemporary design and protagonists of the modern bathroom.

How to furnish a modern bathroom (lighting)

The lighting of a modern bathroom must not be too bright or too dark, but it is necessary to create the right atmosphere to create a relaxing environment and bring out all the furnishing accessories.

For the lighting of the modern bathroom, LED lights are particularly suitable, which can be positioned on the ceiling, recessed, or suspended and which allow you to create light points where necessary such as above the mirror or the shower.

Chapter 15: Masonry Bathroom

— ◆ ◇ ◆ —

Masonry bathroom, better classic or modern?

Those who undertake home renovations and intend to make every room of the house particularly elegant, almost always consider the possibility of having a masonry bathroom built. It is an almost obligatory solution for those who love to take care of even the most marginal aesthetic details of their home and, above all, want to give value to every corner and room.

Masonry bathrooms are an extraordinary alternative to common bathroom furnishings: they are very beautiful to look at, but also functional because they are durable and easy to clean, and able to adapt to all the tastes of those who live in the house, with a style classic or more modern. What makes the difference above all are the different materials, from marble to concrete or wood, used for the coverings. In any case, an excellent result is guaranteed in terms of design and visual impact.

The advantages of a masonry bathroom

Masonry bathrooms seem to have no age, never go out of style. The advantages of this type of solution are many. First of all, there is the possibility of designing them according to your needs and making them perfectly in line with the style of the whole house. Each masonry bathroom is unique and unrepeatable in its way if you choose particular coverings or decorations or ask the designer for a specific arrangement of shelves, structures, and furnishings. The masonry bathrooms allow a sort of personalization of the environment and at the same time optimization of the spaces. They are always very resistant to wear, to shocks, to humidity, and for this reason, they also guarantee a long life.

Classic masonry bathroom

A masonry bathroom is almost always characterized by its ability to give the whole environment a very marked stylistic imprint, regardless of the colors or the choices regarding materials and details. As we said, this type of solution allows you to adapt the bathroom, which is always an environment for which you are looking for great functionality, in an optimal way to your preferences, and personal tastes are in the end acting as a needle of the scale in a choice between classic and modern.

A classic style masonry bathroom is preferred by those who do not like particularly refined furniture. Usually, you opt for a masonry or concrete structure covered by tiles or marble with the sink hole in the upper part, and the tiles and marble also cover part of the wall up to the wall units and the mirror.

If you follow the classic style, the coating is not very innovative but this does not mean that attention to detail is avoided or elegance is given up, there is always a need for meticulous work to make the best choices to make the bathroom aesthetically pleasing. The design is more traditional but we do not give up on a touch that may surprise. In the decorations, in particular, mosaics and ceramics are widespread, which can create an extraordinary glance. With the help of an interior designer, you can find the best solutions for compartments and shelves, for doors, drawers, frames, wood, and more.

The rustic masonry bathroom often made for country houses, is characterized by walls, stone blocks, or rough tiles, always with very warm colors. There is also the country style, sometimes also chosen by those who live in the city to differentiate themselves from the bathrooms that are found in most urban homes.

Modern masonry bathroom

The solutions for a modern masonry bathroom are obviously those closest to the latest furnishing trends. In this case, the use of concrete is widespread for a more minimal, essential, less elaborate, but no less elegant aspect of the environment. Often the washbasin is located inside a masonry piece of furniture, which is then enriched with shelves for storing linen and objects.

Also in this case the furnishing elements and finishes, as well as the materials, play a fundamental role. In the modern bathroom, warm colors are rare and make room for more neutral ones. Resins can be used instead of majolicas, while the sanitary ware, in this case, is suspended, often have a square shape, and have no decoration, unlike classic bathrooms. Something similar is noted for the taps, the design is simple, here too the shape is more squared, and there are no decorative elements, except for a few small details. The tub becomes part of the masonry, but the possible choices for the showers are different. You can also prefer a masonry shower, as if to create a new relaxing environment, in others a glass shower accompanies the entire remaining part of the masonry bathroom.

Masonry bathroom (how to make it with certain times and costs)

The masonry bathroom is a solution that cannot be ignored for those who intend to renovate their home, change its appearance and make it more welcoming, aesthetically pleasing, and functional at the same time. You have to discover the solutions available to furnish the room, from modern or classic bathroom furniture to the available options for sinks, showers, and tubs, and then expose your idea to the designer.

Chapter 16: Classic Bathroom

◆ ◇ ◆

A classic is a book that has never finished saying what it has to say, "If you want to give your bathroom a warm, intimate, and romantic atmosphere, the classic style is the right one for you. A return to the past that has never been set but resurfaces with elegance and refinement."

When furnishing your home, the bathroom is one of the most difficult environments to treat. This is the room in which each of us seeks our intimacy, detaches ourselves from the hard daily routine to indulge in moments of pure relaxation and well-being.

From walls to decorations, from bathroom fixtures to service furniture, we will propose you a journey into the classic furnishing of your bathroom. Grab a pen and paper, and write down everything we are about to tell you.

Coverings and tiles

Classic bathroom coverings. The first step is to choose the right coatings. Always remember this principle: the classic bathroom must amaze, involve, fascinate with its refinement and elegance, guaranteed by the refinement of all the elements that compose it.

When choosing tiles for your bathroom, you need to select high-quality materials. You could opt for marble, a perfect element to combine with the furnishing elements. The white color would give brightness to the whole environment, the perfect combination of harmony and poetry. If marble is not your preference, your choice could fall on porcelain stoneware, ideal for its versatility and ease of maintenance.

As for the floor, on the other hand, you can also opt for a darker color than the walls, to create a pleasant and not excessive contrast.

Sanitary and Taps

As for the selection of sanitary ware, there is little room for choice. The dictates of the classic style bathroom furniture almost impose the choice of free-standing sanitary ware, with a rounded or oval shape, in white and cream colors (even if white predominates).

Classic bathroom fixtures are appreciated precisely for their adaptability, ideal to combine with any furnishing element, the result of a design that will never go out of fashion. For the sink there is only one choice: it must be in white ceramic, embedded in the wooden cabinet.

As for the taps, brass taps are preferred, in bronze and silver color. A leap into the past with soft shapes and three or stronger elements, just as it happened many years ago. Technological developments have made it possible to combine tradition with innovation, guaranteeing high-quality taps, destined to last over time and to exploit all systems for saving water.

Bath or shower

Bathtub with free-standing installation. The bathtub is the characteristic element of the classic style bathroom, the undisputed protagonist of the furniture. It will be a unique piece, with a sinuous and light shape, suitable for creating moments of pure romanticism and intimacy.

Imagine those antique bathtubs, which you've always seen in movies and always dreamed of. Here, the dream can come true. The golden rule for choosing the bathtub is the retro taste. This represents relaxation, escape, the most intimate dimension of the house but it must surprise.

Classic style bathroom furniture

A must in the classic style bathroom furniture is the wooden cabinet on which to fit the sink, accompanied by a mirror in silver leaves. Wood is the primordial element of the classic style, no other material can be chosen.

Chapter 17: The Industrial Bathroom

◆◇◆

A re you open-minded and not afraid to experiment with new things? A bathroom furnished with an industrial style design is the one for you.

What defines an industrial-style bathroom?

The industrial design is minimalist characterized by essential furnishings, dominated by the contrast generated by the use of different materials and often by large sinks that act as a focal point.

A contrast between copper or gold with matte black is a simply ingenious design touch. To recreate the industrial atmosphere it is necessary to make use of raw materials, almost without finishing. It may seem strange to consider concrete as "trendy", but if mixed with the right furniture it can give an extraordinary aesthetic to the rooms of the house.

WHAT MATERIALS DO YOU NEED FOR AN INDUSTRIAL BATHROOM?

Bricks

The appearance of a factory gives you the idea of something robust and essential. You should immediately take care of making the walls with facing bricks. These bricks are perfect for bringing an industrial concept into a bathroom.

The combination of brick with marble becomes exceptional, two very different materials with completely different textures but whose combination works perfectly in an industrial style bathroom.

Concrete

It's amazing how this seemingly cold and unattractive material can turn heads when applied the right way. You can use it for sinks, countertops, walls, and floors. Of course, the use of the walls is what best characterizes the industrial style of a bathroom. The concrete will create a modern effect but also a luxurious atmosphere.

Copper

This luxurious-looking material is a simply stunning detail in an industrial-style bathroom. Neutral tones, combined with matte black, are extremely elegant. Gold finishes and exposed pipes create a whimsical whirlwind of sensations and add character to the bathroom. Just ask a plumber for advice to best realize the idea.

Marble

A truly elegant industrial material for walls and floors. If you think the concrete is too cold, the maxi marble panels are an excellent solution to create a relaxing environment with clean lines. The ideal is to alternate the gray tones of the marble with the white of the porcelain of a freestanding bathtub.

Stone

The living stone gives warmer tones to the bathroom without compromising the industrial style. Particularly suitable for the washbasin that acquires personality and becomes a truly eccentric element.

Steel

The trend in industrial-style bathrooms is to add black steel frames to the showers to create a very obvious focal point in the bathroom.

The shower becomes the protagonist of the environment, with a sharp contrast between the black steel frame and the white of the floor tiles. If you add to all this the steel chrome plating on the handles and light points, the perfect industrial atmosphere is created.

Wood

To add charm, character and a "raw" touch there is nothing better than wood because it warms the environment and creates a beautiful contrast with colder materials such as steel, concrete, or brick. With wooden materials, you can create a "fusion" typical of the urban style.

The coverings that characterize the industrial style of the bathroom

The industrial style bathroom can be both fresh and airy and gloomy and dark, depending on your taste. Coatings are instrumental in strengthening the industrial atmosphere. Let's see which are the best solutions:

Gray concrete tiles: Anthracite gray is an ideal choice when you want to adopt an industrial style for your bathroom. Large dark concrete tiles, covering the floors and walls, create a sense of relaxation and spaciousness of the space.

Vintage porcelain stoneware tiles: Porcelain stoneware tiles are made with a much finer clay than ceramic, making the tile compact and durable, perfect for master bathrooms. If you love industrial vintage, choose white porcelain stoneware with geometric patterns. The taps of the sanitary ware must instead be in matte black, as well as the handles of the furniture, the frames of the mirrors, and the lamps. For the floor choose tiles featuring black and white geometric designs that create a contrast of colors adding charm to the room.

Wood effect tiles: They can be used on bathroom floors and walls. Ceramic tiles create the illusion of real wood. Unlike the latter, they do not deform with humidity or with changes in temperature and are much more resistant. This wood-tone solution is ideal when a warmer industrial atmosphere is desired.

Metropolitan style white tiles: Classic white subway tiles is a must in industrial design. In the bathroom they can be combined with dark gray hexagonal tiles on the floor, creating a modern and refined contrast.

Stone walls: Everything becomes natural with a stone wall. There are several varieties of stone on the market: slate, granite, travertine, sandstone, and marble. The stone walls convey the idea of texture and immediate relaxation.

Chapter 18: The Scandinavian Bathroom

◆ ◇ ◆

candinavian-style furniture has established itself on the market by offering furniture and accessories for the home with functional and harmonious characteristics, in line with the needs of contemporary life. Nordic style bathroom furniture is the latest trend: the sanitary fixtures take on simple and essential shapes while the taps use elegant designs, inspired by the tradition of the past. Here we give you some tips on how to furnish a Nordic style bathroom.

Nordic style bathroom furniture: characteristics and distinctive traits

Its distinctive features are functionality, which can be found in shapes and structures, and simplicity, it also can be found in surfaces and colors. Despite its essentiality, the Nordic style furniture does not renounce elegance, focusing on light, luminous, and timeless ceramic bathroom coverings, which recall the genuine and spontaneous atmospheres of the past. If a few years ago the trend was to hide the structural elements of the bathroom, for example by using a modern bathroom cabinet integrated with the sink, on the contrary, the Scandinavian-style furniture enhances them, leaving the water pipes exposed. The bathroom fixtures have essential geometries and contained sizes: a very useful thing, especially for small bathrooms. The taps are strictly metal and with classic but minimal shapes. Finally, even the furnishing accessories must be characterized by functionality to meet daily needs. Towels and bathroom products are left exposed and displayed on shelves and open furniture, which leave nothing to the imagination but focus on comfort and hospitality.

How to furnish a Nordic style bathroom: some tips

Bathroom tiles

First of all, it will be necessary to standardize the bathroom floor and wall tiles. In fact, this style of furniture favors the use of bathroom tiles and flooring of the same material and color. White ceramic is undoubtedly the best choice to highlight the simplicity and functionality of the Scandinavian bathroom.

Bathroom taps

The Nordic style bathroom taps must be made of metal, preferably unpainted and with natural colors. Also, prefer traditional models with knobs to integrated ones.

Sanitary

Choose a small round or oval sink, to be fixed on a basic metal base or a modern bathroom cabinet. The shower area must be without the tray and the drain will be installed on the floor. Finally, the bidet should not be present, considered a superfluous element in the Nordic style.

Bathroom furniture

As anticipated before, the bathroom furniture must be simple, clean, and linear. The recommended colors are mostly neutral. Exposed wood is allowed, but not in too dark shades. As for other colors, it is better not to overdo it and settle for just one bright shade.

If possible, avoid inserting too many doors or cabinets, towels, washcloths, and other bathroom accessories that can be perfectly displayed.

Nordic peoples have a propensity for practicality and functionality, this is why, even in the bathroom, every accessory, every complement must have its function to facilitate our daily routine.

White and wood effect

You can choose wooden shelves to organize towels and hygiene products and a wall-hung washbasin cabinet. **Please note:** always use light colors (also in combination with black).

Wood gives comfort especially in a room where you take a shower or a bath. Without giving up the grain and beauty of wood, we can opt for porcelain stoneware with a wood effect (water-resistant ceramic material).

Another peculiarity present in many Nordic bathrooms is the boiserie or the coating of the walls that reaches an average height (right above the sanitary ware).

Total white

A detail that can be found in many bathrooms, not only Scandinavian but also across the Channel, is the small rectangular white tiles with dark joints. The honeycomb pattern is also widely used for wall or floor coverings.

The bathtub in a Nordic style bathroom is preferably freestanding, not recessed, while the shower has its separate box. The colors are always clear and the tub is strictly white.

With the harsh climate of the areas close to the Pole, in a hot bath, where a sauna is not possible, it gives the body a regenerating numbness.

The black and white contrast

Often in a Nordic bathroom black is also used to contrast the light tones. Usually, it is the radiators, or rather the towel warmers, that are black in color and recall the old industrial pipes even if of course they are of a very new concept. But a touch of black can also be under our feet with slate-colored planks.

A touch of green

The last two peculiarities of a Nordic style bathroom are a touch of green and the thin and oblique legs of cabinets or washbasin basins. A plant or a call to greenery can never be missing.

Chapter 19: Furnishing The Bathroom In Perfect Feng Shui

How to furnish the bathroom in Feng Shui style? How to choose the right colors and furniture? We have collected for you the most useful tips and rules to follow to create a bathroom according to this ancient spiritual discipline.

Feng Shui, literally wind and water, is a spiritual discipline of Chinese origin, dating back to about four thousand years ago, which intertwines personal well-being with furniture and architecture, to identify the optimal characteristics to create a living space that improves the existence of the people who live there, increasing their relaxation, harmony and success, both personal and professional. It sees the two natural elements as protagonists (wind and water, in fact) which identify themselves in the forces of yin and yang and, according to Asian culture, bring prosperity, health, and happiness.

The fundamental principle is that the house is a living being, characterized by flowing energy and that there is a relationship between this energy and our well-being. Its design must be carried out harmoniously because everything contributes to modifying the energy flow, the orientation of the rooms, the furnishing accessories, the shades, and the materials must be selected according to precise rules. To achieve all this, we use the Bagua (literally "ba", eight and "gua", trigrams) a symbol, or rather a map, which practically translates the principles of Feng Shui, placing a Tao in the center of an octagon and anchoring the eight trigrams to the cardinal points: by doing so, it will be possible to extrapolate the perfect arrangement of all the rooms of the house in order to best support the energies that flow there.

Choosing Feng Shui for the bathroom

The orientation and the furnishing of the bathroom have the great power to influence the well-being of the people; this room is a place to be dedicated mainly to relaxation and self-care and the rules of Feng Shui from the arrangement of the furnishings to the choice of materials, in order to exert a positive action on the energy of the person. It means creating harmony and positive energy within the home.

The rules for furnishing the bathroom according to Feng Shui

In the bathroom, the natural element that predominates is water, a symbol of life, purification, and energy, a source of prosperity and wealth. It is essential that it can flow without hindrance, to ward off negative energies in a continuous regeneration; for this reason, the shower, the bathtub, and the sanitary fixtures must always work perfectly.

According to Feng Shui, the bathroom must be distant both from the kitchen, where the central element is the fire, and not placed in front of the entrance; this, according to some, is due to a question of energy that from the entrance would flow into the house and would be immediately "discharged" in the bathroom; but it is also common sense, as it is neither elegant nor pleasant to be greeted by the cleaning and draining functions as soon as you enter the house, immediately encountering the bathroom door.

Consider diversifying the bathroom (where to wash), the toilet, or toilet (for evacuation activities). The two functions should be separated, both for confidentiality and to avoid disharmony. So choose a small room to insert the toilet and bidet, adjacent to but separate from the bathroom.

The orientation of the bathroom in Feng Shui

Feng Shui recommends orienting the bathroom towards the North, making sure, as we have already mentioned, that it is not communicating with the kitchen. The fire, the main element of this environment, coming into contact with the bathroom would cause a conflict with its alter ego element, water, causing dispersion of energy. When designing the spaces of the house, keep in mind that having a bathroom not adjacent to the bedroom will avoid disturbances during the hours dedicated to sleep.

Avoid placing the bathroom also in the central area of the house, because it is the point in which to let the energies circulate freely unless it is only the washing area (in ancient times the center of the house often housed a patio dedicated to these activities).

The colors of the bathroom in Feng Shui

For the colors, it is advisable to choose the shades of blue, light blue, and light blue, which are also suitable for the bathroom walls. We do not use red and bright shades that recall fire. While green, white, and gray can be used.

The shapes and furnishings of the bathroom in Feng Shui

Prefer soft, wavy, and sinuous shapes, avoiding square and angular ones. The tiles are perfect with patterns that recall the waves and the flow of water, which, observed in series, create movement. Orient yourself on rounded and rounded furnishings, and for the furnishing, materials opt for ceramic and wood, which balances the effect of water.

If you need to renovate a bathroom, without being able to choose its position inside the house, you can intervene by using objects and materials that rebalance the energies: brass and metals in general, for example, are excellent for a bathroom facing south, because they mitigate the activity of the fire element that characterizes this area, and which would be an impediment to water.

For a bathroom in the ground area (Center, North East, and South West) avoid the natural inhibition of water by using marbles, which are characterized by fire energy.

Another fundamental feature for a perfect Feng Shui bathroom is the essentiality of the environment, so aim to eliminate all that is superfluous, leaving only the bare essentials visible. An excellent piece of furniture is scented candles for a calm and welcoming atmosphere.

Mirrors and paintings for the Feng Shui bathroom

Mirrors in the bathroom are indispensable, as they are considered a source of strength and certainly fundamental in self-care, but be careful and do not place them opposite each other, because you will cause a loss of positive energy. You can also hang paintings and images of mountains or rivers, adding a natural component that will help you regenerate and relax in the activities related to this space.

In Feng Shui philosophy it is important to emphasize objects that traditionally bring prosperity and wealth. You could also use in the bathroom, for example, a jewelry box, to store precious objects such as jewelry or ancient coins.

Lighting in the Feng Shui bathroom

Choose natural light to illuminate the bathroom, making sure that there is at least one window, possibly wide; by doing so you will follow the rules of Feng Shui and your bathroom will seem bigger, especially if its size is smaller. Avoid dark shades for curtains and fabrics and you will give the environment a natural airiness and brightness. In case you have a blind bathroom, insert a mirror outside the door, which will activate the otherwise weakened energy, interacting with the internal mirrors; choose a lighting system in warm tones and multi-layered, with at least full-spectrum lights, to counteract the darkness caused by the lack of natural light; of course, you will insert a fan that helps the environment to remain healthy and fresh.

Plants in the Feng Shui bathroom

Plants are perfect elements for a Feng Shui bathroom; of course, they will have to be true, precisely because living beings can interact with the energies of the surrounding environment. They also add elegance and warmth, contrasting the essentiality of the furniture.

The soil of the pots, properly treated with water and spare parts, will be a valid ally in countering bad smells. Choose plants of tropical origin, naturally accustomed to resisting in hot and humid climates. If the bathroom doesn't get a lot of natural light, opt for aloe vera, bamboo, begonia, fern, ficus benjamin, and orchid.

Chapter 20: The Tropical Bath

◆ ◇ ◆

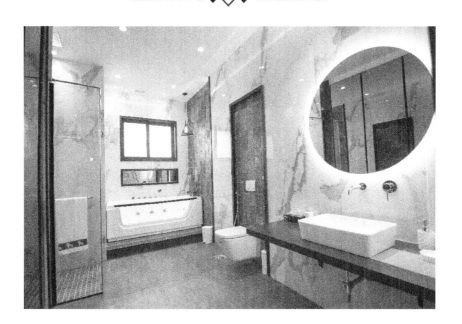

Tropical style bathroom:

colors and movement

How to furnish your bathroom in a tropical style? Here are the most suitable choices from colors to perfect plants. A certainly original way to furnish your bathroom is to use a tropical style, with real plants and flowers, or simply in textures. Being an uncommon choice, here are many ideas on how to adopt this style.

Tropical style bathroom: how to make it

It is now common knowledge that including plants in your furniture leads to many benefits: from keeping the air clean to filtering toxins to promoting a general sense of freshness and well-being in your home. Thanks to the dissemination of this information, it is always easier to find accessories suitable for a green furniture, to be combined with your plants to complete the tropical style. So here are some ideas to take inspiration from.

Shower or bathtub

A large white tub is recommended, if you wanted to recreate a "waterfall" effect, to feel even more immersed in the tropical style, you could opt for a shower with a waterfall jet.

The most suitable colors

Colors characterize the tropical bathroom. For the floor, stick to light tones, with beige, gray, or light brown tiles, creating a mosaic that recalls the colors of the earth. For the walls, you can decide to remain neutral, and then indulge yourself with the green of the plants and other accessories, for example, the shower curtain or for the windows, or resort to particular patterns for the wall tiles, or use pink paint pastel or green.

Better to stay on white furniture, in order to create a very clear contrast with the rest of the furniture, which will show off a perfect tropical look, thanks to the choice of plants and other patterns on the tiles and walls.

Tropical style bathroom: which plants to choose

Here are some examples;

Bamboo

This plant loves to be in humid environments and needs partial exposure to the sun's rays. It is therefore perfect for the environment chosen in this case. It should not be wet too often, but it needs regular pruning.

The Dracaena

This specimen, on the other hand, speaks for itself: it transmits its state of health by changing its color. For example, if the sheets turn yellow or start to fall off, it means it has been too wet. It should be exposed to indirect light.

The Yucca plant

One of the best plants to keep indoors, this plant needs low maintenance and is a top choice when it comes to keeping the air clean. Moreover, thanks to its shape it will perfectly recreate the tropical style you are trying to achieve.

Chapter 21: Exotic Bathroom

T he tropical or jungle style is an eccentric, colorful, wild style, which immediately transmits good humor, love for travel, and a strong and decisive personality. Yes, because furnishing a home with exotic plants, colorful textures, ferocious animals and tropical details is not something for everyone.

Even more so, if it comes to furnishing the bathroom, a room that usually tends to be furnished in a rather classical way. If in the past, the bathroom was the most neglected part of the house or the one in which to invest less energy, today the trend is completely different because the bathroom becomes a place to pamper yourself, relax, and take care of yourself, a place that furniture lover cannot afford to ignore.

Furnishing the bathroom in a jungle style (characteristics)

The first characteristic of the jungle style is the presence of bright colors, which recall tropical palettes, in which green and its many nuances certainly stand out but also red and its undertones, white, yellow, black, brown, Violet. Certainly, the jungle palette is rich and allows you to indulge yourself in mixes and matches.

The second characteristic of the jungle style is the presence of exotic animals: parrots, jaguars, elephants, giraffes, zebras, monkeys, without forgetting the flamingo, so loved that it gives life to a real style, the flamingo style. In short: you can indulge yourself in this sense. Animals can camp on the wallpaper, on small details such as vases, cups, ornaments, printed on curtains, sheets, pillows, or even as real statues, if you have enough space.

The third characteristic of the jungle style is a green light to plants, real or fake, leaves, even printed, exotic fruit, such as pineapple, cactus, and so forth.

The fourth characteristic of the jungle style is the presence of wood, which mixed with the green of the walls, plants, or other details, gives the impression of being in the middle of a forest. The most suitable type of wood for this purpose is bamboo, but you can also play with other types of wood, of course.

1. **Fill it with plants**

   Recreate your green jungle by literally filling your bathroom with plants, the most suitable for this environment are naturally succulents, but you can also go for fake plants. A simple idea but with a sure impact.

2. **Use wooden furniture**

   Here is another simple idea to instantly recreate the impression of being in a lush forest: use wooden furniture. The effect obtained, especially by mixing furniture with neutral colors, such as white and gray, is surprising. The choice of tiles is also fundamental. if you have the possibility, choose tiles with a linear style, so that the result of the combination with the anything but sober elements of the jungle style is always refined and elegant.

3. **Prints and wallpaper**

   Another way to instantly recreate your urban jungle is to use prints and wallpaper. In particular, wallpaper always creates a very strong effect, especially if used only on one wall, leaving the rest of the walls a neutral color, such as white or otherwise natural. If you don't want to dare with wallpaper, then go for prints and checks the jungle effect is guaranteed!

4. **Bamboo and wicker details**

   As we said, wood, especially bamboo, is a great way to give any environment an exotic atmosphere, but wicker baskets do their duty too. In the case of a bathroom, you are spoiled for choice. Here are some examples of bamboo and wicker bathroom accessories. Mats, small containers, baskets, storage boxes choose them in bamboo or wicker for a guaranteed exotic effect.

5. **Minimal**

    Finally, it is not certain that to embrace the jungle style one must necessarily lean towards eccentricity and an over-the-top style at all costs. You can very well love the clean lines and minimal atmosphere and, at the same time, decorate the bathroom in a jungle style. For example, tropical motifs in the coverings, but only one portion (such as the bathtub, or the shower wall) and leaving everything else white. The jungle effect is guaranteed as well as sobriety and elegance.

Chapter 22: Victorian Style

——— ◆◇◆ ———

The Victorian-style makes explicit reference to the design born in the United Kingdom in the mid-nineteenth century and rapidly spread throughout Europe.

Created to meet the needs of the wealthy classes, whose exponents wanted to give a touch of class and refinement to the bathrooms of their elegant homes, it is still today synonymous with refinement and good taste.

The Queen Victorian bathroom (tub)

The furnishing objects that most characterize the Victorian style are undoubtedly the bathtub and the bathroom fixtures. The tub can be in cast iron or enameled steel (but recently acrylic tubs have also been seen) has a sinuous shape, prominent edges, and sumptuous lion's paw feet, made of aluminum or brass.

Victorian style bathroom fixtures

Naturally, English-style bathroom fixtures must also contribute to the creation of a retro atmosphere together with the bathtub.

The "shell" shape and the elaborate foot are the unmistakable elements of the Victorian-style bathroom fixtures. A touch of class can be given by purchasing a seat in mahogany, walnut, or simply black, so that it can stand out against the white of the porcelain.

The Victorian style taps

With three holes or single holes, chromed or brass-plated, the important thing is that both the taps and fittings are "in style", with the white porcelain handle or the typical cross motif. In the more traditional series, there is even a double-tap, one for hot water and one for cold water.

The toilet cistern with backpack or chain

The box deserves a separate discussion: It can be a backpack with a white handle or a high one, with chromed piping and the typically visible chain.

The coatings

In a typically vintage bathroom like the one we are building, even the coverings and floors have their importance. The boiserie is undoubtedly perfect: easily recognizable by its height (100-120 cm) and the use of closing friezes and decorative skirting boards.

The white or burgundy tiles (one of the most popular colors at the time) of small format (brick type) with diamond or hexagonal shapes are also perfect, but black and white chess was also widely used.

Contemporary design

One of the most original trends in contemporary design is that of the contamination between apparently irreconcilable styles. If you manage to harmonize everything, it is not a gamble to insert a Victorian-style piece of furniture in a modern context or to choose furnishings that recall that style without necessarily being vintage.

Chapter 23: The Poor Art Bathroom

◆◇◆

I n the search for the winning formula, in terms of bathroom furniture, many consumers ask themselves the same question, will I be able to create an original room if I opt for a more classic style?

In this chapter, we will show you how to furnish the toilet through the dictates of poor art. By following our advice you will get an effective result, which can bring nostalgic and avant-garde people together.

Arte povera

(characteristics of an all-Italian style)

In Italy, since the second half of the sixties, there has been an interior trend capable of evoking, at first glance, the familiar and popular atmospheres typical of this land. It is the poor art, a fascinating combination of material and tradition, where the taste for simple things becomes the distinctive feature.

The expression "poor art" derives from the homonymous artistic movement, which developed in the same years, which fought consumerism with strokes of visual anarchy, trying to exalt the "poverty of art". This was intended as a return to the elementary principles of nature and the use of primary technological devices.

Today when we talk about poor art furniture we immediately think of a set of anonymous and unkempt old furniture. It is a wrong idea as this style embodies a real design trend, inspired by the rural and peasant world while maintaining painstaking attention to detail.

Adopting it, therefore, does not mean loving the old or the demodé, rather trying to recreate an eternal work of art. If you have always dreamed of a timeless, elegant but charming bathroom, poor art is the right choice for you!

How to create a perfect poor art bathroom

Poor art is usually preferred to furnish the most lived-in rooms of the house, such as the kitchen and the living room. It fits perfectly into any living space, including the bathroom.

The advantage of a rustic style bathroom is its welcoming character. Thanks to the soft shapes, the formality of the accessories, and the warm and enveloping nuances, it is ideal for both the master bathroom and the service room dedicated to guests.

Furthermore, preferring modest elements par excellence, it will not affect the functionality of a lifestyle similar to the sensitivity of the contemporary world. We propose below the elements to consider to create your poor art bathroom.

1. **Colors, floors, and coverings (wood is inevitable)**

    When starting the design of a poor art bathroom, one essential element must be taken into consideration solid wood. It prevails both in the constructions and in the nuances, as it gives immediate warmth to the environment. An excessively rustic atmosphere can make you get too close to the Tyrolean style, clearly different from poor art.

    To select the colors properly, consider the structural characteristics already present. For example: if the ceiling is crossed by large natural beams, choose a wall color in a creamy white, which will help you enhance its beauty without weighing it down.

Forget about any bright and vibrant color. The most suitable color range covers all the candid shades such as beige, white, off-white, pastel green, or antique blue, very trendy. To give an original touch to the walls it is possible to create decorations using stencils. Be careful to select them, however, in perfect harmony with the rest.

The coatings represent an important element. If you have chosen to paint the wall canonically, you can play with country-style tiles in reduced sizes, in blue, amber, green, or brown colors. You can leave the wall bare if it is made of fine stone or light-colored brick. Another possibility concerns the coatings in wooden planks that embrace the entire perimeter of the room. But be careful the wood paneling can darken the room.

For flooring, parquet is usually preferred, such as that of ash, cherry, or walnut. A marble floor, on the other hand, will give the idea of a highly refined mixture of styles. The environment will be less rustic and more luxurious. A tiled background, on the other hand, is the cheapest but equally valid choice for poor art.

2. **Sanitary ware is classic**

    Seductive refinement is the common denominator of this style and touches any piece of furniture, even bathroom fixtures.

    In this case, we can make room for other materials such as porcelain. This is worked to exhibit soft and sinuous shapes, definitely far from those of the modern style.

The bathroom fixtures rest strictly on the ground and the preferred colors are white and light beige. For an effective result, you can have the toilet seat made with the same physical characteristics of the furniture, in wood, of course!

3. **The sink and the poor art furniture**

View of the wooden cabinet with sink set in brass inside a bathroom furnished in poor art, above a large mirror as an accessory. furniture, naturally they too rhyme with the word wood. As a rule, if the size of the room allows it, we opt for spacious and welcoming furniture, such as those we found in the most classic of early twentieth-century homes.

The original color of the wood is not always maintained: sometimes it is subjected to a long process to obtain the ideal shade. Light green or white is very popular. Unlike the modern style, inlays and decorations on the doors are welcome.

If decapé is chosen, it is important to let the grain of the wood be seen which, even when reproduced with industrial techniques, must give the idea of craftsmanship. The finishes, be they matte or glossy, therefore, must be as natural as possible.

Very often other materials are combined with wood. In this regard, the marble top is splendid. The sink (or washbasins, given that the double service is frequent in the master bathroom) is almost always embedded in the piece of furniture that supports it. Ceramic washbasins are preferred, which can also be used for the door knobs. For an original and refined solution, instead of the sink, you can use a beautifully aged brass bucket.

For faucets, brass is the preferred material and the most classic shapes are cross shapes, ideal for giving an antique allure.

The main piece of furniture (the one on which we find the sink, so to speak) is always accompanied by a large mirror, enhanced by worked or essential frames depending on your taste and the chosen furniture.

Instead of the wooden piece of furniture, wrought iron support without doors can be used, with matching objects in sight. It may be poor art, but it's super chic!

4. **The tub is a must**

In poor art, the exceptional must-have is the most classic among the accessories intended for a personal bathtub.

The golden rule for choosing the bathtub is the retro taste. This represents relaxation, escape, the most intimate dimension of the house but it must surprise.

A good idea is to be inspired by the Old England style, where the tubs rest on lion's paw feet, blending the rigor of the Victorian style with the rounded shape of the seat, to favor ergonomics.

To give a touch of personality, you can choose the material contrast: porcelain tub and brass feet. A result of a true fashionist!

5. **Warm lighting**

Illuminating the bathroom is always a fascinating topic. As for natural light, it is a good idea to make sure that the curtains accompany it, to suggest a magical and relaxing atmosphere.

In poor art the positioning of artificial light is strategic. The illuminating point is found in the famous mirror with applique. These pendant lamps resemble the shape of a flower and are made of satin glass or ceramic, with arms in brass or wrought iron.

If you want to amaze, without sacrificing simplicity, you can shed light by inserting a candle in an old glass jar, an excellent idea to give new life to used objects. Finally, the yellow bulb lighting is suitable for emphasizing the idea of warmth in the room, already welcoming in its own right.

6. **The accessories sought after**

To make your poor art bathroom truly unique and irresistible, you can use highly distinctive decorative elements.

A natural wood stool will add charm and elegance to your space. It is a small object but it has an inexplicable decorative potential. A truly delightful idea is to recover an ancient ladder with wooden rungs, it will become the ideal towel holder.

For accessories, choose glass or ceramic depending on the material used for wall lights and washbasins. A beautiful porcelain basin on a wrought iron tripod will immediately attract attention and the dispensers will thus become iconic design pieces.

In cases where space is abundant, you can also insert a column, with glass doors and drawers. There are never too many places to store objects!

Chapter 24: The Mediterranean Style Bathroom

♦◇♦

Would you like to furnish your bathroom in a Mediterranean style? But are you wondering which color to choose for the tiles? Or what materials could you use?

The Mediterranean is sea, warmth, simplicity. A bathroom decorated in this style takes you back to summer and its holidays, to the sound of the waves crashing on the shore, to the lazy sunny August afternoons. What are the most suitable color combinations? Which materials match best? Let's find out together.

1. **Furnishing a Mediterranean style bathroom (wallpaper)**

   Wallpaper can be the star of your Mediterranean-style bathroom. To get the effect of Mediterranean decor, choose it with a blue floral pattern with a white background. Care must be taken that the material it is made of is resistant to moisture. The bathroom is an area of the house where the continuous use of water requires special care.

2. **Furnishing a Mediterranean style bathroom (blue)**

   Blue is undoubtedly the most used color, although not the only one, to compose a Mediterranean-style bathroom. Its dark tones alone are capable of evoking the unfathomable depths of the sea. You can use this nuance in its many shades, such as light blue, blue, and indigo. You can use it for tiles, ceiling painting, and accessories.

3. **Furnishing a Mediterranean style bathroom (sumptuous)**

   The Mediterranean also means culture, that of the Roman people who dominated Europe from the 1st century BC. Here the bathroom is enriched with precious marbles and columns, with a pendant chandelier with encircled arms. Do you love classic and opulent environments? Do you think the bathroom should be the place for your luxurious relaxation? You can use dark wood furniture and a lighting system with elegant glass shade sconces.

4. **Furnishing a Mediterranean style bathroom (orange)**

Not just the shades of blue. Orange can also be a perfect color for your Mediterranean-style bathroom. Go for its lighter shade to get the effect of the light of a sun setting at the sea on the distant horizon line. Use it in tiles with a natural light-boosting effect. For sanitary ware, choose traditional models with a thin foot.

5. **Furnishing a Mediterranean style bathroom (tiles)**

Unmissable protagonists of the bathrooms at home, the tiles must be made of materials that do not absorb water, such as stone, ceramic, stoneware, or terracotta. To obtain a Mediterranean-style décor, the ceramic ones in their shaded blue version recall the white foam of the sea that dissolves into a thousand bubbles. The effect is gentle for a cozy bathroom with a delicate character.

6. **Furnishing a Mediterranean style bathroom (step)**

The step in the bathroom is a decision sometimes taken for aesthetic purposes, sometimes the result of necessity, such as the need to obtain a perfect slope for the sanitary drains or to facilitate the use of the bathtub and shower.

In any case, its scenic effect is undeniable. A Mediterranean-style bathroom has a triumphal trait in it. In its sumptuous version, it leaves simplicity and rusticity behind, to become more brazen.

7. **Furnishing a Mediterranean style bathroom (beige)**

An elegant version of a Mediterranean-style bathroom sees beige as a discreet and delicate ally. We find it in the painting of the walls and in the flooring, which can be declined with tiles in a darker shade. Further soften the arched window effect with white fixtures, candles, and a wrought iron table with a subtle design.

8. **Furnish a Mediterranean style bathroom (marble)**

Scenic and delicate at the same time, marble with its veins and colors has a classic trait. A Mediterranean-style bathroom can be furnished with this material that takes us back to the Roman Empire era.

Arabescato white marble is a type that has very intense dark veins and is extracted from the area of the Apuan Alps and Versilia. It can be used for floors, to cover furniture shelves, and even on the wall to highlight a certain area of the room, such as that of the shower.

9. **Furnishing a Mediterranean style bathroom (white)**

White is the color of purity and cleanliness, both qualities that a bathroom must possess. According to. Use it in furniture that has a classic design with a Carrara marble top with lightly marked veins. Even the tiles can be colored in this neutral shade. Give character to the environment with furniture with a more particular design, such as a mirror with a golden frame.

10. **Furnishing a Mediterranean style bathroom (light)**

Light is a typical feature of Mediterranean environments. The sun shines almost all year round. For your Mediterranean-style bathroom, play with the light effects of a window to recreate a sunny habitat at home.

Use white in the wall and floor tiles to multiply the sparkles. Complete with turquoise, light blue, and light blue furnishings such as tablecloths, curtains, and flowers.

The Mediterranean style bathroom can be declined in a rustic version embracing simplicity or have a more sumptuous character in its reference to the classical world. The colors of the sea, light blue, light blue, blue, but also beige, white and orange are well combined. Among the most suitable materials, we find marble, wood, and wicker.

Chapter 25: Bathroom In Shabby Chic Style

◆ ◇ ◆

S habby Chic furniture affects every room of your thing and to give a unique and unmistakable style to every room our advice will be very precious.

As it will be clear to you by now, the shabby chic style is so versatile and customizable, that we can enrich it with those particular elements that we consider indispensable and that depend on our needs and our taste. Great attention must be paid to colors, chromatic shades, and, last but not least, to the general furnishings of the house.

The shabby chic style allows you to furnish your bathroom in the great economy creativity is the eco-carbonate of this enchanting and refined style.

Buying the Ikea furniture to be stabbed, rather than having it made to measure by a trusted carpenter, or even recovering the mirror at the nearest market, will allow you to experiment with your creativity never losing sight of the fundamental coordinates, to create a perfect and comfortable shabby chic bathroom, may the photos, attached here, be your guide to make the right choice!

The shabby chic bathroom is perfect if it is combined with total white furnishings or floral-style wallpaper. It's about blending the rustic style with the addition of a French twist and vintage accessories.

Here are some helpful tips

- Paint the walls with neutral colors (off-white, cream, ivory, dove-gray, pastel tones of pink or dusty blue, etc.)
- Choose furniture that apparently may seem "old and worn" but which for this reason are perfectly suited to specify the shabby bathroom furniture;
- You can also opt for an eclectic mix of different styles in wood or metal, accessories such as the soap dispenser or the towel hanger.
  plaster friezes can revive a French or Scandinavian atmosphere, creating a very elegant and sophisticated environment.

The vintage bathtub is a must, not only does it make the bathroom look luxurious but it will be the glue of the assortment of furniture as a whole. If it has ornate feet and friezes all around it can perfectly reflect the shabby chic charm.

- Finally decorative bathroom accessories, such as glass jars, small floral prints, and pretty lavender candles.

Shabby furniture to decorate your bathroom

Of course, when you decide to furnish a bathroom it is not possible to neglect the furniture that must be rigorously shabby. Now I'll explain why. Beyond the kitchen, there is another room in the house that you love to take care of down to the smallest detail; from curtains to accessories, from multi-purpose containers to toilets, and this is the bathroom. This room also represents a business card of the house and of those who live there. So never underestimate it.

Some furnishing accessories can never be missing in a shabby bathroom. Let's start with the ladder, it is an indispensable element. You can choose it in any color, certainly, if you opt for a wood color you will reach the top, especially if the whole environment is all white. You can easily place it on any wall and it can become a beautiful towel holder or a unique hanger for your bathrobes. Or it can simply stand there waiting for the most suitable use.

The shabby furniture accessories for the bathroom

We then continue with the mirror. The size does not matter, as long as it is romantic and with very delicate decorations; then if you have a bathroom large enough instead of the classic mirror you can also consider a toilet, you know how nice to place not only perfumes and tricks but also the wonderful shabby containers that you have made for example with anonymous glass jars to contain sponges, wadding.

If, on the other hand, you have always wanted one of the shabby bathroom furniture that is also a container, choose it low, in pastel colors, and with frosted glass doors. Hide what you don't want to show or what you didn't have time to fix. You can also pickle it or paint it yourself, possibly always in tune with the rest of the environment.

Do not forget, however, the wicker baskets, especially if they are white or rope-colored, which you can place just about anywhere, even under the shabby-style bathroom wall unit always if they are high from the ground. Otherwise, you can also place them under the sink or near the tub or next to the window because you know that in the shabby world there is no limit to the imagination. For glass containers make makeup brush holders.

These are small tips that are only good if you want to wash your bathroom face, thus avoiding upsetting it or doing major renovations. However, nothing prevents you from using these ideas to have a sort of guidelines, especially if you do not know how to furnish it or even how to embellish it, once the work is finished. In the meantime it starts, don't hesitate any further!

From Shabby to Country Chic style

(here is how to transform your bathroom)

If you love the shabby style but not its more affected aspect, which is dominated by two fluffy, bulky, and floral fabrics, as well as too vintage accessories, then you should opt for the country chic style.

The country chic bathroom will be a very elegant, almost enchanted environment, in which the color par excellence is a total white declined in pastel shades. It starts from the choice of colors, which enliven the walls and give the room the first decor.

The furniture must be selected according to one's taste but also according to what are the dictates of a very specific style, we said pastel colors, then beige, pink, green, and blue, wooden sideboard, the classic bathtub with feet, tiles in full view thanks to the joints, curtains, carpets and, if there is space, even a retro-style chair.

How to furnish your country bathroom

Leaving a wall, for example, just evicted or with live bricks can be an alternative suggestion for those who want to stand out from the crowd. Based on the general style of the room, you can then choose what is usually defined as furnishing accessories, such as the chandelier, the carpets, the mirrors.

I find this style truly irresistible, it is equidistant from the excesses in which it can easily trespass, it always keeps a low profile and, in the end, everyone likes the result because it is always very elegant. We have therefore said colors and furnishing accessories, accessories, and small tasteful details that can make the difference, such as the choice of fabrics. Don't forget that personal touch that gives the room an edge.

Each element must be coordinated with the other, avoiding that attention being channeled to detail but leaving the overall picture the possibility of capturing attention.

Help yourself in the furnishings by going to low-cost stores

If you are good, you will succeed in this enterprise. If you have to renovate the room, it will be easier for you to interpret the style, if you want to try to get closer without spending a lot, the advice is to start with buying the right accessories also in the low-cost stores, such as Ikea, famous all over the world. Even one detail can make a difference, let alone two.

Shabby furniture has now become a lifestyle that lends itself well to all needs. Whatever the size of your thing you can still choose to furnish it following this style. If you have a small bathroom and a limited budget you don't have to despair. However, with this guide, you can get what you want and what works for you.

It must be borne in mind, before knowing anything else, that the bathroom, compared to the rest of the house, can be furnished in a completely different way. It is the characterizing note that makes the difference. For this reason, interior designers generally choose a different type of floor than the one chosen for the rest of the house.

Shabby chic bathrooms

(how much do they cost?)

Some believe that the greatest cost for the renovation is due to the coating. In reality, this is not the case. Painting could not be a solution, also because the material (stucco, paint, and insulation) has its cost. Instead, it could be useful to rely on large showrooms that often launch advantageous offers, which are worth seizing on the fly. Having established this, let's now go on to list what are the characteristics and elements related to our beloved style.

For shabby chic bathrooms, vintage furniture is essential. They are furnishing elements that are not difficult to find. In fact, just go to a flea market or to a neighbor who wants to get rid of the old furniture to be able to try the deal. However, some chromatic rules must be followed. Prefer warm shades of white or cream or opt for pastel colors.

For these types of bathrooms also consider the choice of bathroom fixtures installed as a pedestal sink. This will give you space to add an old chest or trunk as storage. Replace the steel towel racks and faucets with bronze ones, and use floral patterned tiles behind the bathtub. Paint the walls a warm cream or any pastel color and change the frame around the mirror to a more richly decorated one. Choose a crystal chandelier, even a plastic fake, it adds a decorative vintage touch to a bathroom corner.

Accessories focus on luxury and elegance rather than pursuing, with stubbornness, the shabby or vintage style. Choose robes or towels made of bamboo fabric. They are soft and absorbent, without forgetting the silk which, if enriched with roses, will surely be able to give that tone of luxury you are pursuing. Remember the little details like, for example, the handmade lemon, lavender, or rose soaps wrapped in lace. And then many hearts, plaster hearts would be fine too. Find out how you can make them yourself. Watch the video, it's really easy.

Chapter 26: The Country Bathroom

— ◆ ◇ ◆ —

The bathroom is one of the most important yet most neglected rooms in the house. Like all other rooms, it should have a specific style, which reflects your taste and your needs. Country bathroom furniture is perhaps one of the most popular and most practical styles today. It combines elements of great simplicity with touches of luxury, which add comfort and elegance to the whole.

To the inexperienced eye, the country bathroom looks like an effortlessly furnished environment. It almost seems that the sense of relaxation is a secondary effect obtained by chance. Not so: all the elements of the bathroom furniture - sink, bathtub, accessories - are chosen with care. The final effect is a harmonious and elegant environment, but never formal.

What is country bathroom furniture?

The country-style takes its cue from the rustic houses found in the southern United States and Canada. For many years it has been relegated to country houses, but it is gaining momentum both indoors and outdoors. Here then appear country chic terraces and gardens, but also furniture for the living room and bathroom furniture.

In the country style, natural materials dominate especially rustic wood. The latter might seem like a bit of a strange choice for the bathroom but just opt for quality products. Ceramics and iron are also central materials, which come back both in furnishing accessories and in accessories.

Country chic and shabby chic are often confused. In reality, the two bathroom furnishings are very different, especially in the color choices. A country bathroom tends to favor warm colors such as brown in all its shades, white and red. A shabby chic bathroom will instead tend to be white, dominated by slightly dusty pastel shades.

Enamelled cast iron bathtubs

Central elements of the country furniture are the enamelled cast iron bathtubs, often placed in the center of the room. They have four feet that support them and are much wider than traditional bathtubs. They immediately catch the eye and present themselves as real design elements. Unfortunately, they are also very bulky and unsuitable for bathrooms in today's homes.

A good alternative is a corner bathtub, which takes up much less space and is just as comfortable. As the name indicates, it is a tub wedged at a right angle. On the other hand, it is an inevitable choice in the face of certain sizes. You can make up for this thanks to the rest of the furniture and the use of accessories with a rustic flavor. The corner often results in a shelf or two to be used to hold shampoo and soap, but that's not all. Here you can give vent to your imagination, throwing yourself on the ceramic soap dish, small bathroom accessories in black wrought iron, and plants.

Bathroom with parquet and tiles

The classic materials of country furniture are ceramic and wood. For the first, there are no big problems: you can indulge yourself with the combination of bathroom tiles. The classic hexagonal bathroom tiles are ideal, for example, especially if enriched here and there with floral decorations. Others, on the other hand, prefer terracotta tiles to have a warmer and more comfortable final effect. What to do with wood, though? Better to limit it to furniture only?

While it may seem like a bold choice, a much-loved solution is a bathroom with parquet and tiles. The final result is a bathroom with a rustic look, which recalls the atmosphere of the houses of the past. When you get out of the bath, the floor is warm and welcoming. Everything invites you to relax and let yourself go.

Another solution involves the walls covered with wooden panels. The appearance is somewhat reminiscent of that of spas and saunas. It is a warm design without a shadow of a doubt, but one that has several problems related to the delicacy of the material. The new bathroom tile trends offer an alternative solution: wood-effect tiles. This way you have the design of wood and the merits of a tiled wall.

The new tile trends for the country chic bathroom

But what are the new tile trends for the country chic bathroom? Wood-effect tiles are very popular and in demand, but also those that imitate the effect of stone, with its solid appearance and its purplish-gray shades. Taupe is also a good choice for a country chic bathroom. It goes well with white and with light shades of wood.

Among the new trends in bathroom tiles is the revaluation of visible joints. The plaster space that can be glimpsed between one tile and another has long been considered a limitation in appearance and functionality. Tile joints are difficult to clean and get dirty easily.

The material used to make wood or stone effect tiles is porcelain stoneware, a material with numerous positive characteristics that make it very popular in the construction sector. It is resistant to blows, abrasions, wear due to time, dust and atmospheric agents, chemicals. Furthermore, porcelain stoneware stands out for its good compactness, versatility, and excellent aesthetics.

Built-in or countertop washbasins for the bathroom?

Built-in or countertop bathroom sinks? Both solutions find space in the furnishing of a country bathroom. You can choose the one that best suits your bathroom and the space you have available. The important thing is to combine brown or white bathroom accessories, in natural and somewhat rough materials.

The built-in washbasins are large and can be used in environments of all sizes. You can have them mounted on a natural stone or wooden shelf, for a rustic effect. Otherwise, you can choose a built-in washbasin with a ceramic top and pair it with a wooden cabinet. The wooden cabinet also goes well with the countertop bathroom sinks, which are reminiscent of the washbasins of the past.

If you want a double sink for your bathroom, built-in is the best choice. You can put your soap dish and brushes to the side, for example. The countertop bathroom washbasins, however, are a solution that has been very fashionable in recent years. Small models are also available, ideal for small sizes.

The advantages of the double washbasin for the bathroom

A double sink is a useful object, which is suitable for architectural-style bathrooms. It can also be easily inserted in a country chic bathroom, where natural materials and chromatic notes prevail. It requires quite large spaces and has the charm of abundance.

Owning a double sink for the bathroom has several advantages. It allows you to make up for the lack of a second bathroom or simply to speed up the preparation of family members in the morning and the evening.

With this solution, the small rites of everyday life can be shared, such as brushing your teeth, face, putting on make-up, and shaving. There is no need to wait for your spouse, brother, or sister to finish preparing. The sink is doubled and preparation times are halved.

The minimum space required to mount a double washbasin for the bathroom is 120 cm, but to have the conditions of maximum comfort it is good to consider the structures with a width of 140 cm. Thus, the two basins are of a sufficiently comfortable size to wash without watering the floor and there is enough space to place all the necessary objects for the toilet, soap dish, toothpaste, toothbrush, creams for all needs, and any object deemed necessary.

Black, brown, and white bathroom accessories are suitable for a room decorated in a country chic style. The chromatic notes that characterize them are neutral and perfectly match all the shades of the materials of nature, wood, and stone. Let's discover the possible combinations for a rustic yet elegant bathroom.

Black wrought iron bathroom accessories are small items that complete the harmony of a country chic style room. Their material recalls the correspondences between the rustic aspect of the whole and the world of the countryside, where you live in contact with nature and its rhythms. These are useful, subtle, sinuous small parts that create a pleasant combination with wood-effect bathroom tiles.

Soapdish and toothbrush holders, towel holders, wall hangers, and many other furnishing accessories equip the room dedicated to hygiene and well-being. If they are made as bathroom accessories in black wrought iron they easily combine with materials such as stone and wood. They contrast with the white ceramic while creating visual resonances with the grain of the wood and the mottling of the granite or marble.

Another possible combination for black wrought iron accessories is hexagonal bathroom tiles. The multiplication of lines and the particularity of the shape are softened by the soft volumes that characterize the small objects.

Brown bathroom accessories are ideal for pairing with light or dark wood furniture. In turn, they are made of wood and give a romantic touch to the room. Indeed, wood is a warm material, which arouses feelings of tranquility and harmony with the space that surrounds us. Pleasant to the touch and sight, it is the most popular choice for rooms furnished in country style.

White bathroom accessories allow you to create a pleasant visual contrast with darker furniture, made of wood or stone. If the floor is white or light, they recall its luminous chromatic note and create a pleasant counterpoint of light and dark.

Chapter 27: The Parisian Bathroom

From an anonymous, small, or old-style bathroom, to a chic bathroom thanks to 9 ideas learned from the Ville Lumière. Paris is always Paris, yet sometimes the apartments have that je ne sais quoi that even their inhabitants have innate taste and the ability to give value and character even to small and not always easy spaces. Have you ever noticed how bohemian attics and nineteenth-century buildings, for example, often hide tiny bathrooms in their apartments, with particular shapes, old tiles, and old-style sanitary ware? Yet, what a style!

So, if small or old bathrooms seem to be the mole of your home, here's how to transform them by giving them the charm of a Salle de bain comme à Paris. We learn from the French to give our bathrooms that touch that transforms them from anonymous and small ones to salle de bain with character and style to sell!

1. **Try a large dressing table**

    Does an elegant bathroom in a small space seem like a mission impossible to you? A large mirror with a beautiful black lacquered frame will add depth to the room. Black accessories, the wall painted in dove gray up to half height, and the sponges in a super chic blue-gray color, and... that's it!

2. **Choose an impressive wallpaper**

    How about a slight boudoir bathroom? Cover a wall with wallpaper with toile de jouy motifs, a recurring pattern in the country style, complete with a mirror with a flower frame, and eventually replace the taps following a more retro design, choosing them in brass or rose gold, for example. Furthermore, the idea of adding a splash guard is right.

3. **Get inspired by the old shops**

    Does your new-old bathroom have English-style fixtures? Turn it into a hipster barbershop! Recover an old piece of furniture to use to display all the beauty products, frame the photos of some beauty of yesteryear (in the markets you will find beautiful ones among the old postcards), and choose only white towels, perhaps with your initials embroidered.

4. **Emphasize the retro effect**

Does your bathroom look like grandma at first glance? Accentuate the retro effect by choosing pastel colors and old-style accessories for the walls such as crystal chandeliers, old perfume bottles, and the hunting trophy (perfect for hanging your necklaces or shower cap). And maybe even think about repainting the bathtub in a pastel color.

5. **Use font colors**

   Anonymous bathroom? For Parisians, it is a "no, merci". We do like them: we focus on color, but let it be special! From powder blue to sugar paper, to peacock blue, a Frenchman would have no hesitation! Just remember to choose coordinated sponges and the chic effect is guaranteed.

6. **Create a romantic setting**

   What do you dream of is a romantic bath? If your bathroom is also in an attic, do as it sometimes happens in Paris: keep the old structural beams and if you are not lucky enough to have them, why not?

7. **Choose vintage accessories**

   Check out Instagram: tiles like these are super photographed! If you are lucky enough to have some of the time, keep them, otherwise opt for the new cement tiles. A wicker armchair and stool perhaps recovered in a flea market and updated with new upholstery in a lively color, will complete the "retro and classy bathroom" operation.

8. **Study the shapes and sizes of the bathroom fixtures**

   Have you thought about your bathroom "with this shape how I will furnish it"? Here is sanitary ware suitable for an environment with a particular cut. Remember that the white diamond tile, metropolitan style, in cases like these guarantees a very, very chic result.

9. **Insert a sliding glass door**

If it seems to you that creating a nice bathroom in an attic is an impossible task, here is a good idea: replace part of the partition wall with a glass window and add a sliding door, but all in an industrial style.

Chapter 28: Making An Arab Bath

◆◇◆

How to create the typical Arab bath, a place of relaxation and personal well-being. How to choose colors, materials, and decorations appropriately. The importance of the bathtub. The accessories to make the atmosphere of a Thousand and One Nights.

The sumptuousness and pleasantness of the decorations, expressed in particular in the choice of colored tiles and infinite patterns, make the Arab bathroom environment a room of a thousand and one nights, in which to stop for many hours of the day, taking care of yourself, for the personal pleasure that is often given up.

The Hamman, the term with which the Middle Eastern bathroom is identified, a place of personal well-being where people perform real aesthetic and therapeutic rituals, is made up of several rooms, where temperatures vary to help the body heal from seasonal ills, regenerating.

If in the private home the space is not infinite, it will be possible to recreate a small oasis of well-being by borrowing colors, materials, and decorations, to have the right space at one's disposal.

When you want to have a bathroom in which to relax, the preference for the bathtub is almost obvious. Its presence, preferably a stone or masonry model, ensures great charm you will pleasantly immerse yourself in the evenings when you want to relax.

Great attention is paid to the choice of the covering, with mosaic motifs or arabesque tiles, fascinating textures of absolute value. The presence of an imposing pool is a manifestation of wealth and opulence, which is why accessing it by steps is a way to increase its importance. The large and gilded mirrors, placed behind, are thus further embellishment, a splendid outline.

The materials are different, treated in an artisanal way, an operation that makes them very sensual and personalized. From the marble and ceramic floor to the stone bathtub, naturalness ensures charm in the bathroom.

There is no shortage of fabrics, both for the linen, abundant and well supplied, and for the curtains on the windows and small windows, further decoration. The wood for the small accessories and furnishing components, such as tubs, containers for perfumes, and the laundry basket, as well as glass for the many mirrors, complete the Arab bathroom to perfection.

The play of colors created in the Arab bathroom is essential to have a pleasant and comfortable environment. Feeling good in a room, even alone requires intelligent use of colors which must make the space seem large and avoid that claustrophobic effect that would only reduce the stay in the room so as not to feel suffocated.

The options are linked to personal taste, for those who want an exuberant, lively and cheerful bathroom, it will be easy to opt for shades of blue, light blue, turquoise, green.

The taste for luxury and the splendor of Arab environments provide for the combination of gold with darker colors such as black and brown, in addition to white, beige, and ivory that make the furnishings stand out.

For those who have the possibility and the desire to have walls in Tadelakt, the particular wall covering made with lime, bright and waterproof, it will be fantastic to combine a strong color such as blue, excellent contrast with the clarity of gray and ivory. The black and white mosaic floor is one of the surface coating choices to consider for the perfect Arab bathroom.

For Westerners, taking care of the choice of wall covering is an elegant form of decoration. In the Arab bathroom, on the other hand, it is an integral part of the creation of the room, to which due attention must be paid.

The Arab bath adopts the tadelakt, an ancient lime-based plastering technique that originates in Morocco, and is used to cover the walls of entire buildings in North Africa, as well as for the Arab baths, the Hammam, in which people love to chill out. The characteristic of this ancient working method is the impermeability, deriving from the firing of limestone rocks in the furnaces.

The laying of the tadelakt must be entrusted to experts; it is a technique that requires accuracy and a lot of patience, to recreate a pleasant environment but above all to guarantee its resistance to steam and temperature changes. The mixture is laid on the walls as if it were plaster, worked with river pebbles to make it smooth.

Subsequently, the walls are treated with a black soap based on olive oil, to make them soft to the touch, as well as shiny and waterproof.

The tadelakt is used, as well as for the walls of the rooms, to cover the floors, bathtubs, and the sink. In this way, the absence of escape routes makes the room easier to clean, hygienic and resulting in a modern form of interior design.

While favoring keeping the large spaces in the room, considering it a room that can live on its own and not simply marked by usability, furnishing accessories in Arab culture improve the quality of life and represent a further expression of wealth.

This is why choose elegant, sinuous, and well-worked taps, in the characteristic golden color, which go well with the round shapes of the bathroom fixtures and the washbasin. The mirrors boast particular frames, gilded, finished, with evident decorations, never sober, useful to make these useful objects even more important.

Comfortable cushions to lean against the walls, thinking of a hypothesis of a large bathroom renovation, for those who want a small spa in the home.

The bucket or small wooden tub, from which to draw hot water, is a very rare object in modern homes, but which in Arab countries is a typical element.

The lighting choices are based on the creation of a romantic place with a sensual appearance, accentuating the rounded and blunt shapes of the furnishings, preferring to remain blurred and light, without ever dazzling.

Moroccan suspension lamps, handcrafted and in precious metal, copper and bronze in particular, ensure sensuality, letting the light filter through in a soft way, pleasant even when used to furnish outdoor spaces.

Round and small scented candles, scattered here and there, will become a colorful decoration when you want to relax without looking anxiously at the clock.

Chapter 29: The Zen Bathroom

◆◇◆

M ore and more people are choosing the oriental style to furnish their homes. Whether it is simply decorative elements or rooms completely recreated to recall Japan, the Japanese art in the care of the home conquers a large number of admirers. And, if carefully designed, this style can also prove to be particularly friendly to the environment and recycling, thanks to the use of natural materials, which is added profound respect for the cycles of nature. How to create a bathroom in perfect Zen style as a result?

Before starting, however, it is useful to specify how often in the West the term zen is used in a completely generic way, mostly to identify

Japanese-derived design styles. In reality, this definition could be misleading, as the Asian art of home care derives from the synergy of numerous disciplines. Here are some useful tips.

As already mentioned, in the field of Western furniture the term Zen is used generically to indicate Japanese-derived design styles, without major references to the disciplines that determine their basis. In reality, Zen is a very profound concept linked to Buddhism, based on the search for inner and outer harmony, for a perfect balance of man and the elements within nature. Consequently, defining any home care and beautification work as Zen could be misleading, especially if the term is misused to identify any product of Japanese culture.

Extremely generic, the Zen disciplines try to achieve the perfect balance of natural elements, a symbol of harmony and inner peace. In the care of the home, this concept is expressed with the arrangement of furniture, objects, decorations, and embellishments so that they respect precisely this balance, taking on a symbolic value. The bathroom, in this sense, becomes an emblematic environment of one's home, it can combine the energies of at least three of the essential elements of existence, namely the earth, air, and of course water.

Also from a theoretical point of view, Zen bathrooms tend to be characterized by minimalism and essentiality, therefore they are devoid of objects and decorations that could be excessively superfluous, even suffocating, in the search for balance. Then prevail wooden floors, white ceramics with simple lines and warm colors but with dark shades. Furthermore, the elements are positioned in the room so that their energy is not contrasted, moreover the reference to nature is strong with decorative elements that can remember it on a symbolic level, such as pebbles and stones.

To create a Japanese-inspired bathroom, therefore "Zen" according to the common language, it is useful to start from the flooring. Wooden floors should be preferred, possibly dark brown, made from long panels of considerable width. Not a simple parquet, therefore, but real planks, smoothed and made opaque. The same color must be chosen for any furniture to be inserted in the environment: it is better to prefer medium-height drawer cabinets, directly positioned on the floor, or cabinets built into the wall, possibly with sliding doors with opaque glass panels.

One of the most characteristic elements of a Japanese bathroom is the inevitable screen, to separate not only the tub area from the rest of the bathroom but also to recreate a place of privacy for undressing and putting away your clothes. For this reason, depending on the size at your disposal, you can place more booths in the same room. The traditional one is the shoji, a screen made of dark wood, whose peculiarity is the characteristic opaque white or beige squares.

The bathtub is also of great importance, as it is very different from the one usually available in European homes. In the Rising Sun, it is not unusual to resort to square or rectangular tubs, positioned at floor level or, again, a little higher. The perimeter of the pool itself, often characterized by low mosaic or wood-clad walls, is often surrounded by a layer of round pebbles, a reference to nature but also an important solution for water drainage.

Finally, on the decoration front, simple and monochromatic walls are preferred, possibly embellished with imperial-inspired paintings or lithographs, as well as ceramic vases with gold finishes. moreover, do not forget how the bathroom requires a good presence of green plants with large leaves, to rebalance the energies of the water element with those of the earth element.

Chapter 30: The Resin Bath

Have you heard of resin baths? Are you interested in understanding why many people are thinking about it? Resin in the bathroom is a modern and hygienically perfect solution. As we will see in the course of the chapter, it is a material with many advantages even at an interesting cost.

Once the resin was used only in the industry. The evolution of modern resins allows excellent use even in our homes. The classic use in the home is for bathroom renovation.

Opinions on the pros and cons of resin are to the advantage of the pros, even compared to the cost of being able to cover existing bathroom walls and floor tiles without demolition.

Let's explore together the theme of a resin bathroom (pros, cons, and costs)

The cost of a resin bathroom can vary from € 50 to € 150 per square meter without accessories or bathroom fixtures. The variability of prices is very wide and depends on the type of resin chosen and the cost of the installation for the covering or the resin floor.

For example, between a colored resin and a spatula with a wood effect, the price varies from € 30 per square meter, then if you switch to decorated resins up to those with a 3d effect you can get very high prices.

Another cost factor to redo a resin bathroom is its initial state. If it is possible to spread and lay the resin over the bathroom tiles without demolishing the existing one. In this case, the height of the wall also affects the cost per square meter.

To find out the real price, ask for several quotes to make a resin bathroom from many specialized companies in your area and compare the different offers.

Resin is often used to cover tiles because it allows the job to be done without having to remove the coating and prepare the wall. The use of resin for this type of use is very common.

To cover the tiles of a bathroom with resin, the average cost is from € 50 to € 100 per square meter. This variability depends a lot on the technique of laying the resin and on the state of the initial wall. The cost of the material alone is around € 40 per square meter.

Ask for a quote to cover the tiles with resin and find out the real cost after meeting with different companies.

Resin bathroom walls (prices)

As we have just seen, the use of resin for walls is very widespread. For the walls, generally, only one type of resin is used to be applied 3 times. Compared to a floor, the price for the bathroom walls is lower. The advantage, as we have seen, is to be able to cover the existing covering without having to demolish the tiles. To make resin bathroom walls the price is around € 40 per square meter for the resin.

Resin bathroom floors (prices)

An advantage of the resin is its very low thickness. Having a coating thickness of only 3 mm allows you to create a resin bathroom floor on top of the existing one without problems for door openings or others.

Compared to use for floor coverings the situation is slightly more complex and expensive. Generally, several layers of resin must be used;

- The first layer of support.
- A second layer with the resin of the color chosen for the floor.
- A third final layer of transparent resin for protection and anti-slip treatment.

To make resin bathroom floors, prices start at € 50 per square meter for the self-leveling resin only, including all materials. The considerations made previously apply to the installation. We can assume at least € 80 per square meter for a complete job.

For both a floor and the walls of the bathroom, ask for a free and no-obligation quote for a resin bathroom from various companies specialized in resins, obtaining offers to evaluate and compare after meeting the companies.

When we talk about the pros and cons of a resin bathroom, opinions can be of various kinds and the central theme is the use of resin in private construction. But opinions and judgments are changing especially for a bathroom redo.

Until a few years ago they made it perfect for industrial use but not very usable in the construction sector. In recent years, the evolution of materials and various laying techniques have made the resin perfect in the private building sector and in particular for bathroom and kitchen coverings.

The main opinions on the advantages and pros of using resin in the bathroom are:

- Obtain bathrooms that are easy to clean and hygienic thanks to the quality of the resin being waterproof, water-repellent, and the absence of mold.
- Resistance to shocks and chemical agents that can fall on a bathroom floor.
- The resin can be laid over the bathroom tiles without having to demolish the existing ones thanks to its minimal thickness.
- Colors and shades of various types, from spatula to glossy up to decorative effects such as 3D floors.
- If you have underfloor heating, the resin is a problem-free material.

When it comes to opinions there are also defects of resin baths such as;

- If you don't have the floor treated with non-slip material, you won't be able to stand up in your bathroom. Once installed, the resin is extremely smooth and does not absorb water, so if it gets wet the floor is extremely slippery.
- You can cover existing tiles with resin only if the floor or wall is perfectly smooth. In particular, if you think of self-leveling resins for the bathroom floor.
- The cost of the resin bath can vary greatly depending on the initial state of the bath to be redone and the materials chosen.

Chapter 31: The Smart Bathroom

◆ ◇ ◆

Until a few years ago, home automation was mainly used to remotely manage alarms, doors, and heating. After a while, she also entered the kitchen. In recent times it is increasingly present also in another room of the house; the bathroom. This trend is justified not only to increase user comfort. Home automation in the bathroom also has advantages from an economic and ecological point of view. Thanks to it, it is possible to prevent damage to the pipes or avoid the formation of mold by detecting temperature and humidity. In addition, it allows you to minimize the use of electricity, water, and heating.

So let's see in detail some of the most beautiful home automation solutions for the bathroom.

The "smart" toilet from Japan

The application of home automation to the toilet was born in Japan. Heated seats, controls for the water jet (which replaces that of "our" bidet) adjustable according to the sex of the user and their needs, diffusion of fragrances, and music playback are just some of the options included by the Japanese in their toilet.

There are also "smart" toilets that detect the presence of the person and automatically open the lid or that spray a deodorant while carrying out bodily functions, that play stimulating songs, or that light up at night. Everything is, of course, customizable and manageable also via smartphone.

A relaxing bath even for those with limited time. What's better than a good relaxing bath? Of course, it is not always easy to carve out the time necessary for such an enjoyable activity, and home automation could help in this. Some applications remotely control a control unit connected to the bathtub through a series of sensors. With this system, it is possible to plan, and remotely, when and how you want to take a bath. You can "communicate" to the tub the time in which it should fill, at what temperature, and even the level of density of the foam and the desired fragrance. In this way, in addition to saving energy and water, it will also be possible to reduce the time needed to organize this pleasant ritual.

Home automation in the shower

Even the shower can be a truly relaxing place, especially if home automation systems are applied to it. For example, it is possible to insert panels for managing the strength and temperature of the water jets, but also chromotherapy and music therapy functions. It is possible to insert, integrating them into the showerhead, FM radio, and Bluetooth interface to be able to listen to music from any device. For the more sophisticated, there are also aromatherapy systems with diffusers built into the shower that emit different types of fragrances. In short, with the help of home automation, even a quick shower can become a decidedly pleasant sensory experience.

Google Assistant

Google also threw itself into the remote control of our entire home, thanks to Google Assistant. Through a dedicated app, we can manage everything from the bathtub to the water temperature, from the shower water jet to the bathroom lights. Everything is just a click away.

Light control app

There are numerous apps related to home lighting control. In this case, it is difficult to list them all, as they are developed by those who trade in the relevant bulbs. Philips app, Ikea, or Hive are just a few examples of these numerous application. With this app, we can use them to manage the intensity of the bathroom lights, turn them off if we have forgotten them and vice versa, and, in some cases, thanks to these apps we are also informed of any power surges.

A very complete and multifunctional app is the Kohler Konnect app, which not only allows you to adjust the intensity of the bathroom lights but also the water, pressure, temperature, and set times for shower or tub use.

This digital revolution mainly concerns taps and fittings, with the new mixers which, thanks to home automation, offer top-level performance.

Characterized by a simple but at the same time refined design, excellent quality, and extreme functionality of use, they are perfect for environments with attention to every detail.

Equipped with human-friendly technology, with a single and simple touch, they allow you to interface with water and carry out daily activities even more pleasantly.

In particular, they allow you to electronically customize not only the temperature but also the flow and duration of the water jet for the various functions, to set up to three different configurations that can be traced, then, through the smart memory function and if accompanied by lighting. led, become ideal for real home chromotherapy sessions.

Therefore, thanks to home automation, the modern bathroom increasingly resembles a spa, capable of creating a total form of well-being that does not neglect environmental protection, contributing to the saving of energy and water resources.

Obviously, the aesthetic side is not put aside, on the contrary, it remains in the foreground, offering captivating shapes and refined elegance.

The home automation mixers have a bold, sometimes futuristic look that cannot be overlooked, becoming a part of the sink, or rather a real digital interface to it.

Digitization has now also reached the bathroom and allows you to enjoy new comforts at the push of a button. With the electronic taps, the sound system for the bathroom, and the different types of lighting for the bathtubs and whirlpools, you can indulge yourself.

Especially those who consider the bathroom as a place of relaxation where to recharge their batteries want to be able to customize the atmosphere and comfort according to their individual preferences: a perfect water temperature in the bathtub, their favorite music, and pleasant lighting. , all adjustable in the simplest way possible: with a finger.

A standard was already available for many modern bathrooms, which combine aesthetics, comfort, and functionality.

Music and sounds accompany our life and influence our moods.

The integration of an audio system with the bathtub, therefore, constitutes an important step forward in research on the bathroom environment.

Immerse yourself in a sea of light and colors

The positive effect of light and colors on the body and spirit has been known for centuries, which together with water can offer an even deeper level of relaxation.

If the technological possibilities are endless, the bathroom of the future will be beautiful, sustainable and will not lose its emotional component

True consolidated trend, technological innovation is, increasingly, a friend of comfort and efficiency: at the service of well-being and health, it fulfills the wishes of those seeking relaxation and a moment of perfect, intimate peace.

Home automation and digital devices are now, in fact, able to transform the room at a simple touch according to every need. They are already in fact facial recognition systems that automatically adjust the water temperature, the amount of light, and even the type of music depending on the person who enters the room; bathtubs that fill themselves at a set time or when they receive input from the smartphone, bringing the water to the ideal level and temperature;

mirrors that allow you to connect directly to your mobile phone and on which, in the future, you could read the news, check the weather or watch TV. And some take it a step further, imagining smart mirrors capable of monitoring the health of those in the mirror and transmitting the relevant information to the referring physician.

It's still. Thanks to technology, the latest generation faucets will allow perfect adjustment of the percentage of hot and cold water and, if equipped with a dynamic flow regulator, will reduce consumption by up to 50%. There are already digital recirculation showers that purify, heat, and use recycled water through a closed circuit which, therefore, promise savings of up to 90% of water and up to 80% of energy. And digitized showers with voice activation capabilities are being developed that can be started remotely and can be equipped with waterproof TVs.

And how is design evolving? Few matching tone-on-tone finishes, essential exposed structure, great space for geometries: a clean and essential design that enhances shapes, colors, materials, and textures. Washbasins, furnishing accessories, and furniture confirm the general trend towards customization. Sanitary fixtures and fittings will be increasingly minimal, rigorous, with almost mathematical features and reduced thicknesses. The mirrors will act as co-stars: the mix and match of shapes will replace the large circular mirror in vogue for some time; will come walls made of mirrors with shapes reminiscent of origami; mirrors with shelves, towel rails, and lighting sensor and mirrors with an integrated light that is more and more emotional. The propensity towards delicate nuances will continue but solid colors will also emerge, enlivened by bold lines in contrast.

If the technological possibilities seem and are infinite, the bathroom of the future will be really beautiful but above all, it will not lose its emotional component: the room dedicated to the self will remain, where you can find the balance between body, mind, and spirit.

Chapter 32: Tips To Save On A Bathroom Remodel

— ◆ ◇ ◆ —

There are so many bathroom renovation projects that can be found online, but when you renovate your home, the cost of renovating the bathroom is always one of the highest, especially due to the presence of water-sanitary and electrical systems: For this reason, a guide that can allow you to carry out bathroom renovations while keeping your budget under control is very useful.

Remodeling a bathroom without demolishing: tips for walls and floors

One of the most concrete ways to save by renovating the home bathroom is to avoid demolitions (provided clearly that the aforementioned systems are still in good condition) since they represent the most incident expense item when it comes to renovating a bathroom: let's see how to make a change of look without removing the tiles.

The first solution is represented by the use of ultra-thin floors and walls that can be glued directly on the old ones. Among the materials that can be used to renovate bathroom floors without having to demolish are listed below;

Stoneware: in the slim version, it has a thickness ranging from 4.8 to 6 mm and is characterized by resistance, lightness, ease of cutting, fire resistance, eco-compatibility, and simple maintainability, as well as installation on both ceramic and stone elements natural or marble.

The resin with a very low thickness (3 - 4 mm), despite its thinness (although a 0.5 mm fiberglass mesh is also included which has the function of reinforcing, reinforcing, and sealing the joints of any underlying flooring), the Thin resin floors are resistant to compression, chemical aggression and are easy to clean

The adhesive laminates (3 mm) to be applied dry on existing coatings are characterized by lightness, flexibility, durability, and great aesthetic effect. When it comes to renovating the vertical walls of a bathroom economically and practically, it is easier to use.

Bamboo fiber: a 100% natural three-dimensional coating, easy to assemble, light, sound-absorbing, impact-resistant, and chromatically versatile

Ultra-thin solid wood slats to be glued with specific products directly on the screed or floor below, which are then subjected to a subsequent treatment that ensures stability and durability over time.

3D decors: we are not just talking about wallpaper in the bathroom, but also about adhesive tiles.

Two-component epoxy enamel: in this case, the tiles must be treated with a water-based fixing insulator and possibly with an anti-mold liquid, then with an anti-condensation heat-insulating paint and an acid solution that degreases and thoroughly cleans the old tiles; lightly sand and spread the enamel (prepared with its catalyst) using a brush, working on small surfaces and insisting above all on the joints between the tiles; a roll is then passed to make the surface uniform let it dry.

Renovating the bathroom while keeping the budget under control is also possible by implementing other measures, including changing the old and encrusted taps, difficult to return to their original state.

Whether it is polished or satin steel, matt black or brass, with a cascade jet, with a round or square shape, you are spoiled for choice.

But be careful when you decide to change the old taps to the new model, not only because some of the above products are not cheap at all, above all because it is necessary that the connections are the same otherwise there is a risk that a trick to restructure the bathroom in economy turns instead into a very salty plumber's fee !!!

Renovate a bathroom without spending a fortune: replace the sink and bathroom fixtures. If you are not satisfied with just replacing the taps, it is advisable to install new washbasins and sanitary fixtures.

Even for the washbasins, there is no limit to the imagination: column, suspended (with or without half-column), free-standing, countertop, built-in, semi-recessed, integrated into the top; and also in ceramic, glass, stone, white, or colored.

Is it possible to renovate the bathroom while saving money and changing the bathroom fixtures anyway?

Yes! It is possible to renovate the bathroom while saving money and changing the bathroom fixture.

Bathroom furniture: how to save money in the renovation by recovering old furniture, or by using "original" raw material, or by resorting to do-it-yourself.

Renewing by adding salvaged elements is a way not only to safeguard the wallet when renovating the bathroom at home but also to guarantee a very fashionable effect from the old trunk to the antique table, from the mirror to a lived-in ladder. Crates take the place of shelves and furniture with open compartments.

Do not immediately think of buying the ready to use because it will be enough to recover those of the fruit and vegetables, clean them, sand them and paint them if you have a minimum of familiarity with do-it-yourself.

Pompeian red and white bricks for a retro glamorous bathroom, of which we also invite you to appreciate the cabinet on which the sink was placed, which most likely was originally located in some entrance.

A reclaimed basin becomes a perfect washbasin for a bathroom with an antique flavor. An old zinc basin takes on the convenient function of a large sink.

For those who are familiar with DIY, another possible intervention is the painting of the furniture, perhaps using colors following the shades of the floor.

How to renovate a bathroom while saving money (focus on accessories)

If you renovate a bathroom economically, after repainting the tiles and changing the bathroom fixtures and sink (or perhaps omitting these steps if the budget is very tight) you can move on to trendy accessories and furnishing accessories, whose materials range from rattan (for example for the laundry basket) to wrought iron (used for towel bars or lamps to hang on the side of the mirror), to hyper-colored plastic (for the toilet brush), passing through steel, below are some of the web accessories that most intrigued us.

Cheaply renovating a bathroom (is it possible to also replace the bathtub with the shower?)

However, if you want to replace the old bathtub with the shower, even if it is an economic renovation of the bathroom, you will have to budget at least 1500 euros, even if the costs will depend on the quality of the materials and the type of shower you choose to use.

Why change the tub to a shower?

This is because it is cheaper, ecological, and faster, allowing you to save water and space (especially essential in a bathroom that does not have large sizes, the most recent models are synonymous with relaxation. Many opt for the replacement of the tub with a shower also for reasons of accessibility, especially when there are elderly or disabled people in the house.

Removing the bathtub implies that some parts of the floor and wall will remain without the covering, how do you manage in these cases when to save money on the bathroom renovation you cannot or do not want to completely change them?

The solutions are;

1. Replace the tub with an identically sized shower
2. Have a custom shower built, using the tiles left over from the first assembly

3. Use mosaic on the uncovered parts. Speaking of mosaics, even without the need to change the tub, it can still give the touch you were looking for in a bathroom to be renovated while saving money because it brings color and liveliness to the configuration of the space.

4. Apply a contrasting material (or even the same but in different colors, or with different poses)

5. Mount wall panels, which perfectly embellish the void left by the tub.

6. Renovate a bathroom with small touches and tricks without spending a lot (indeed sometimes spending very little)

7. If your bathroom has a bad floor but you don't have enough budget to change it, a large carpet can hide the problem.

Bathroom floor renovation with carpet

A new chandelier or wall light lanterns with candles, plants, a new shower curtain, a mirror with a particular frame. Even with the mirrors, you could decorate entire walls, a combination of different shapes and sizes broadens perspectives and width naturally and remarkably.

One other essential thing that should not be overlooked is plants, which enliven the atmosphere with a natural touch, capable of livening up the atmosphere of the bathroom without spending much.

Finally, don't forget the windows that can be transformed with colored glass, decoration, and liveliness for a fairly low cost.

Ways to save money on a bathroom renovation

1. **Paint The Tiles Instead Of Removing Them**

   To eliminate the existing coverings, it is necessary to detach them (and/or split them) piece by piece. This operation has a huge impact on the cost of renovating the bathroom and on the total hours of work.

   You can cover the tiles with specific materials Redoing the bathroom without removing the tiles is a perfect idea to reduce costs.

2. **Place the new floor tiles above the existing tiles**

   Again, without breaking the entire floor, it is possible to renew the style of the bathroom with new tiles in a contemporary style: The tiles are applied on top of the existing ones.

   Do you know that "redoing a bathroom without removing tiles" is one of the most searched phrases on Google? It must be a widespread necessity (considering the cost of total bathroom demolition).

3. **Maintain the position of the elements without intervening in the pipes**

   Keeping the original arrangement of bathroom fixtures and furnishings allows you to greatly limit your total expense. It will be enough to disassemble the old pieces and install the new ones.

In this case, be careful to check the drainage of the new sanitary fixtures, it must be compatible with the position of the original holes.

4. **Bet on a few decor elements**

   With taste and clear ideas on the style of the bathroom, just a few pieces of furniture are enough to redo the bathroom in a new and modern style.

Printed in Great Britain
by Amazon

80123881R00108